Leather Tramp
Journal

Josh Broderick
4/22/02

"Rich Broderick's **Leather Tramp Journal** *invites us on a journey — a journey into the deep recesses of the soul and toward the vast expanses of the cosmos. This 12-mile retreat of wonder and wisdom is a promise of transformation. Enjoy the journey and come back changed."*

—**Jim Conlon,** Director of *Sophia Center* at Holy Names College in Oakland, CA, Author, *Ponderings from the Precipice* (Forest of Peace) and *The Sacred Impulse* (Crossroad)

"If you don't have time now to take a long ramble through your favorite wilderness, Rich Broderick's **Leather Tramp Journal** *can substitute. Trek along with him and share in his ruminations about spirituality, God in our midst, living a full and meaningful life and a hundred other things worth thinking and talking over."*

—**Rich Heffern,** Author, *Daybreak Within: Living in a Sacred World* (Forest of Peace) and *Adventures in Simple Living* (Crossroad). Rich is on the editorial staff at the *National Catholic Reporter.*

Leather Tramp Journal

A 12-Mile
Mountain Retreat

Richard Broderick

illustrated by
Karl Gehring

FOREST OF PEACE PUBLISHING • LEAVENWORTH, KS

Leather Tramp Journal

copyright © 2001, by Richard Broderick

Library of Congress Cataloging-in-Publication Data

Broderick, Richard, 1940-
    Leather tramp journal : a 12-mile mountain retreat / Richard Broderick ; illustrated by Karl Gehring
        p. cm.
    ISBN 0-939516-55-1 (pbk.)
        1. Retreats. 2. Spiritual life—Christianity. 3. Spiritual life—Catholic
    Church. 4. Nature—Religious aspects—Christianity. I. Title.
BV5068.R4B76 2001
269'.6—dc21   2001023166

published by

Forest of Peace Publishing, Inc.
PO Box 269
Leavenworth, KS 66048-0269   USA
1-800-659-3227
www.forestofpeace.com

printed by
Hall Commercial Printing
Topeka, KS 66608-0007

illustrated by
Karl Gehring

1st printing: July 2001

This Journal is Dedicated to

all my friends who have journeyed with me
through the seasons of change in my life.

Some friendships have begun in the few miles of recent years. Others have walked with me the long miles of many years. Their constant and abiding presence has given me strength to make it through the deep ravines and intensified my joys by celebrating with me on the peak experiences of life. Their gifts of encouragement, acceptance, love and prayer have enabled me to grow, take risks and believe in my dreams.

I am grateful to the faith community of St. Thomas the Apostle, Delmar, NY, for establishing a strong foundation for future ministry and for the years of laughter and fun shared together. I am grateful to the Latin American communities I have served. They have taught me to keep my finger on the pulse of life and to live each day. I thank the North Country communities of Blessed Sacrament, Hague, NY; St. John the Baptist, Chestertown, NY and St. Teresa of Avila, Brant Lake, NY, for their bold collaboration in shaping new vibrant, inclusive faith communities that have put backcountry parishes on the cutting edge of renewal. I express gratitude to the faith community of St. Mary's, Crescent, NY, that nurtured interest in a "global parish," leading to life-giving relationships with parish communities in Guatemala. Thanks to the faith communities of San Pedro, Jocopilas, Santa Cruz del Quiche, and San Lucas Toliman, Santiago Atitlan, in Guatemala for their courageous witness of living the Gospel in solidarity with the poor and for being silent heroes of peace. Thank you to Sr. Frances Eustace, CSJ, retired professor of English at the College of St. Rose, whose keen mind cleared away the underbrush of errant syntax from the literary pathway of this Journal. And to Tom Skorupa, editor, who with gentle persuasion saw and drew forth material that was resting at the depth of the pond of the mind, making something good even better. I express gratitude to my parents and extended family for providing more than just a base camp for my life but rather provided a home where selfless love was given every mile of every day. I can only poorly repay all by my lasting gratitude. All of this confirms the axiom that it takes one writer to thank an entire village.

I went to the woods because I wished to live deliberately, to front only the essential facts of life and see if I could not learn what it had to teach, and not, when I came to die, discover that I had not lived.

—Henry David Thoreau

Contents

Introduction

Henry David Thoreau once wrote, "I went to the woods because I wished to live deliberately, to front only the essential facts of life and see if I could not learn what it had to teach, and not, when I came to die, discover that I had not lived." For many years I have been living with a desire to do something like what Thoreau did at Walden Pond. I've wanted to step back and take a long look at my fifty-eight years of life. I've wanted to address some of the *quintessential spiritual questions* that keep coming to me with the constancy of the tides, to face into these questions without distractions.

Where is life for me? This is the most constant and persistent question I live with. It flows frequently, like a spring, into my consciousness. Other questions follow in its wake: *Does what I am doing have any real meaning? Is it life-giving for me or anyone else?*

I realize that I have lived more years than I have left to live. This gives focus to the amount of time, energy and life I have left to give to a cause or to others. *At this stage of my life, what really matters? What inside of me still wants to come to life?* These are some of the first questions that arise.

I first came upon the term *leather tramp* in John Krakauer's book *Into the Wild*. He labeled what I wanted to do. A leather tramp is described as one who puts on hiking boots and goes off into the mountains for long treks alone. They are distinguished from "rail tramps" or "auto tramps," who use rail or cars for transportation.

Taking long treks alone as a leather tramp would let me explore both the mountains and the topography of my soul. So, at a key juncture in my life I requested some sabbatical time. Then I put on my hiking boots and left for the Adirondack Mountains, carrying nothing but my backpack and these quintessential questions that have been composting within.

When I stand on a ridge after a little climbing, I often stop and view the sunny peaks in the distance. I can look below into the valleys and get an overview of my journey. Taking time out from treadmill living gives us the opportunity to look at the peaks and valleys of our lives and to note where the settled and silent memories of our past lay. These peaks and valleys tell our story.

This leather tramp journal is simply an open reflection of one trekker on a pathway of life still haunted by a purpose, still wrestling with his angel. This leather tramp is a seeker of spiritual pathways that will fill the soul with more appreciation for life's gifts and give strength to meet life's challenges.

This journal is also an invitation for you to read the important trail markers along the path of your life and to make the decision to live more deliberately. A line from Mary Oliver's poem comes to mind: "What am I going to do with the rest of my wild and precious life?" This is a question worth spending time with.

These reflections may not lead to a redistribution of the world's wealth. But if they help to redistribute my priorities and change some of the unthinking patterns of my daily life, then it may encourage you to put on hiking boots and take a look at the topography of your soul.

My hope is that this 12-mile, 12-day mountain journal will give you encouragement to walk your own path of life, which is never clear but which only comes into view by trekking mindfully, one step at a time. On my own trek I don't expect that I will be knocked off my horse by a blinding flash, nor do I anticipate that answers will appear in front of me with the suddenness of a desert sunrise. I can only describe what impels me to begin this journey as a feeling that has accumulated into a force. It pushes me onto a pathway that does not have clear markers and toward a destination that has not yet come into view. My best hope is that I will gain a new perspective on my life, on what I feel called to devote myself to — for as many miles as I am given to walk during my remaining lifetime.

Mile One

A Journey Begun

Journey is a word sometimes used as a metaphor for our life on earth. It connotes meaning and purpose rather than distance traveled or years lived. The question is commonly asked, "Where are you on your journey now?" It's a way of asking, "Where and how are you presently engaged with life? What's going on within your soul?"

This backpacking journey that I'm about to embark on isn't just about reaching the *Flowed Lands* — a valley in the Adirondack Mountains — at the end of this day, nor is it getting to the *Upper Works,* my destination at the end of this 12-mile trek. It has more to do with exploring the inner landscape of my soul. Fundamentally, its purpose is to address the quintessential question, "Where is life for me now?"

As I gather my hiking gear from my car and prepare to begin this leather tramp sojourn, I reflect on what has moved me to take up this journey now. Recently, I have sensed a change of seasons taking place in my life. For some time I had been discerning movements within my heart suggesting that a change was needed. I was losing the flow of life in my ministry and was beginning to feel a sense of dread. Six years as pastor was filled with a range of emotional highs and lows, challenges and changes, acceptance and rejection. I was committed to preaching a social Gospel using a *charismatic* style of leadership, one that is spontaneous, intuitive and energized by a vision of what we could become. I wanted the community to be more global and environmentally aware, more inclusive of the marginal and those who had been alienated by past pastoral practices. I was critical of church doctrine that excluded women and frowned on experimenting with new paradigms of pastoral planning. All these aspects of my ministry were attracting newer members but alienating some older ones. I realized that the direction we were taking as a pastoral team would eventually lead to major conflict with current church directives. Recognizing a need for a shift, I wanted to be pro-active on my own behalf and looked over the horizon to find something that I could embrace in a wholehearted way. I wanted to find work that would be fun and different and that would enable me to apply all my past experiences and learning. I felt a longing to do something that would make a difference. Only one critical question remained: Where was God now leading me?

I've chosen to spend this questioning time in these Adirondack Mountains in upstate New York seeking clarity. I'm drawn to the crystal clear waters of the winding Hudson River flowing next to the trail. Its source can be traced back to a small brook flowing out of Lake Tear of the Clouds, just below the summit of Tahawus (Mt. Marcy). Maybe I'm trying to trace back to the sources of life that feed into my soul. These mountains have always been a soulful place for me, a place of alluring beauty and mystery. Whenever I spend time in these mountains, I return with feelings of spiritual and physical restoration, deep peace and a sense of gratitude for the gift of my life. In these mountains I always feel uplifted and connected to a sacred natural world. As I begin to climb today, I have a heightened sense of the sacred in this forested cathedral.

Shifting my backpack as I take to the trail, my enthusiasm for the journey is buoyed by the beauty and wonder of this mountain environment. I have always found enchantment in the very name *Adirondack*. It's originally a Native American word. The Adirondacks were originally claimed by two Indian nations, the Iroquois and the Algonquins, who competed in the same area for beaver trapping and who fought over the water routes of Lakes George and Champlain. There has been much discussion about the origin and meaning of this name. Some say that it was a term the Iroquois used (disparagingly) to refer to the Algonquins, who were forced to live on tree buds and bark during the severe winters. A loose translation is *bark eater*. This area was officially named the Adirondacks when Professor Ebenezer Emmons did his first geological survey of the region in 1837, a surprisingly late date in North American history. The impenetrability of the forest had long discouraged exploration and travel. In fact, Lewis and Clark charted the northwest region of the U.S. three decades before the first ascent of Tahawus (Mt. Marcy) and 70 years before the source of the Hudson River was discovered by Europeans.

The rocks making up the Adirondack region are amongst the oldest on the planet, over a billion years old. At one point in geological time these mountains were at an elevation rivaling, if not exceeding, that of the Himalayas. However, what one sees today is the result of the last Ice Age, 10,000 years ago. Ice more than a mile thick compressed, ground and sheared off some of the peaks. The retreating glaciers left behind the giant boulders called *erratics*. These immense boulders weighing tons seem so out of place on top of these high peaks, a kind of practical joke left behind by the glaciers for me to muse on.

In the 1850s the timber industry and iron mines exploited these lands. The iron companies strip-cut the forest to feed their blast furnaces for processing iron ore; the timber industry selectively cut trees to supply the paper industry. I passed the residual of one of these furnaces on the road to the parking lot. It stands as a memorial to a past time. Nature is slowly breaking it down as if to erase the memory of a past trauma. Records indicate as many as a million logs being driven down the Hudson River to the paper mills. While the iron mines never made a profit, the paper industry still hauled logs out of this northern wilderness. Fearing the loss of watershed for the downstate area, a movement began to designate the area as "Forever Wild." A clause to that effect was added to the New York State Constitution by the state's voters on November 6, 1894. Now, as then, controversy has surrounded this constitutional provision. This six-million-acre park is a mix of private and "forever wild" land. Yet, despite its checkered environmental history, many consider the Adirondack Park to be for the East what Yosemite is for the West. As I make my way on this first mile of my wilderness journey, I recall these words of John Muir:

> Thousands of tired, nerve-shaken, over-civilized people are beginning to find out that going to the mountains is going home; that wildness is a necessity; and that mountain parks and reservations are useful not only as fountains of timber and irrigating rivers but as fountains of life.

The "Bark Eaters" survived harsh winters eating tree bark, but for me, a leather tramp, I am hoping to be fed a kind of manna from heaven. Like the Israelites of old, I feel that I can survive this wilderness of the soul and reach a new "promised land" in my life. For me at this time, the journey metaphor is a term for faith.

While I come here during a special season in my inner life, each of the four seasons of the year is a kind of sacramental celebration for me. Each season in the Adirondacks offers a unique, refreshing interior spiritual gift. The green summer season is full of verdant and abundant life. It reminds me of the passage from the Book of Genesis where God looks upon all that God has made and says that "it is all so good." I'm transfixed by the silver-capped water coursing through the flumes and by the warm winds carrying the sound of songbirds and the scent of flowers. Peregrine Falcons ride the thermals in circling spires over the mountains. These long summer days are filled to the brim with sunlight. This season speaks to me of how prodigal, how extravagant, God was with this creation. The uncountable variety of flowers, seeds, growing fruits and vegetables speak of a lavish, loving God who is generous without measure.

The yellow-red-orange-brown autumn season displays a vibrant dance of life before death. Looking down from the mountain peaks toward the harvest arrayed in the distant fields, one is filled with gratitude for life's gifts. Autumn's spiritual gift is conducive for reflecting on the meaning of one's life, as well as one's old age and mortality. It points to the Paschal Mystery of dying and a future rising to new life. The falling leaves teach about letting go; we are not in control of our lives. I find it intriguing that Nature displays her most beautiful colors and blazes with life at a time when she is about to die. Perhaps this happens so that we won't forget her through the winter. Perhaps she teaches us that a timely, graceful death can be a beautiful gift.

The white winter season blows in from the north, shaking snow out of the clouds as they pass over mountains and land. The frigid cold stops the movement of life. As reflected in the frozen ponds, it is a time of hibernation and sleep. The deep, dark nights can reflect our own "dark nights of the soul." We live without the sensual delights of summer. Our senses are low. This is a season of interiority, a time of stillness and repose, a retreat from the surface of life's activity. The snow-saturated mountain forests lead me to an inner place of contemplative prayer, of waiting and quiet listening for the clear, quiet voice within.

The delicate verdant spring fulfills the eternal promise of rebirth. It gifts us with wonder and mystery, as new life-forms break through the winter tomb of earth. It is a time of rebirth and hope, of music and poetry, a time for new beginnings. It is a time for a new spiritual awakening. The dance of life begins again.

The turning of the seasons of nature helps me through all the seasons of my soul — and somehow all the seasons of the year seem to be alive for me during this present mountain journey. I can cope with change and know that life goes on. Dying to my small life plan can open me to a larger one. Dying to my fears and my need for shallow security can cultivate in me a larger trust. The purpose of our small daily dying, I believe, is to open us to a larger life that we could not have imagined for ourselves. At some point in our lives we must stop avoiding the big questions about the meaning of our lives. We must face the choices we sometimes are afraid to make in order to live fully. In one sense, it would have been easier for me to cave in under the pressure of being a "sensible, predictable, likeable pastor," but that type of taming is deadly to the soul. Giving in to such external demands causes us to live someone else's life, not our own. I am leaving behind an ordered, predictable life and going into the future without a plan that I can define. I am not in control.

Yet I feel very much at home as I make my way in this wilderness searching for a Holy Grail. In my "civilized world," I live encapsulated by steel and glass. My daily routines and rituals are performed without much awareness. I can go through the entire day without feeling the throbbing pulse of life around me. There, my life seems so settled and sanitized. However, in this environment of trees, wildlife, wetlands and wild raging rivers, I find refreshment. My sense of wonder is awakened.

I consider our natural environment to be a habitat for the soul. Thomas Berry, cultural historian and theologian, explains this connection:

> The outer world is necessary for the inner world; they're not two worlds but a single world with two aspects: the outer and the inner. If we don't have certain outer experiences, we don't have certain inner experiences, or at least we don't have them in a profound way. We need the sun, the moon, the stars, the rivers, the birds, the song of the birds, the fish in the sea, to evoke a world of mystery, to evoke the sacred.

I have come to realize how much my spiritual life has been and continues to be nurtured in this wilderness. It provides for me a recovery and a recharging of my life force. Conversely, the seemingly ongoing destruction of our natural environment causes me to grieve.

By destroying our environment, we are diminishing the life flow of wonder and beauty into the human soul. The lessening of natural beauty impacts our poetic expression and vision of life. A world devoid of whales breaching the ocean, or a sky without the sight of migrating birds, or a forest without the chant of songbirds or the music of a waterfall makes for a sterile world. Can you imagine our world without meadows full of dancing colorful wildflowers? Without such treasures of nature the greenwood of our imagination and creativity dry up and become as brittle as sticks. We might just as well be living on the landscape of the moon.

I feel there is a strong correlation between the destruction of our environment and the dying of our life within. With more species pushed to extinction (two species every hour, according to *Worldwatch* reports), we lessen our poetic vocabulary and power of wonder. With the diminishment of our color-filled brimming-with-life natural world, our spiritual habitat is equally impacted. That unsettling awareness sends our artistic spirit wandering like a desert nomad looking for a watering hole. The eye of our imagination begins to close; our view of life is narrowed.

If we continue the present rate of destruction, what will be left to inspire us to compose symphonies, paint flowers, write poetry or dance ballet? Would we ever have seen the artistic genius of Van Gogh if starry skies were not visible, if there were no flowers standing in sunlight to paint? I don't think so. A mall will never inspire a musical masterpiece. Another expressway will not lift our souls to the poetic grandeur of a Gerard Manley Hopkins or a Robert Frost. Suburban sprawl like a lava flow is covering over our dark, soil-rich farmlands. We are cutting down orchards and trees to build faster highway systems. Are these not signs of *distress* rather than *progress?* We may get to our workplace faster but at what cost?

The changes in our environment are occurring as quickly as a desert sunrise, yet the long-term effects on the entire earth community are not being adequately considered. A comment by Sergei Skvortsov, a Moscow television reporter, suggests our present state, "We have a saying in Russia: Even the old grandmother does not cross herself until the lightning strikes." We can see the lightning on the horizon, yet as a people we seem addicted to our conveniences and comfort levels. By contrast, I am one who still feels it's better to sit under a large shade tree than in an air-conditioned room.

I think that we are overlooking how much the surrounding landscape affects how we feel. Consider that when the pioneers were moving westward, crossing the Great Plains proved to be the most tedious and difficult part of their journey. Women, men and even the horses became listless and emotionally fatigued. They lost their appetites and energy. It became very difficult to plod on ahead. The monotony of a seemingly endless flat landscape created a boredom and dreariness that drained their energy. It's ironic that the smoothest and easiest travel of their entire journey became the most difficult emotionally. When they were forging rivers or cutting through mountain passes and forests, their whole life force was engaged.

Our communities and cities and highways are all beginning to have the same boring look. We are creating a *Generica America*. The diverse natural landscape is replaced with a monotonous sameness that anesthetizes our imagination. We see the same fast food chains, gas stations and malls everywhere we travel. Our cities are planned to accommodate lots for parking cars rather than paths for bike riding or walking, spaces to play or other activities for people. This white music in the background of our daily life has become like the strains of the Sirens of old. The monotonous droning now lures us not to our death but rather to lives of quiet desperation. We can feel the life-draining *ennui* of the pioneers who crossed the Great Plains.

As I reflect on the pioneers' long odyssey, I decide to take a break after the first mile of my mountain journey. I set my backpack down to rest and listen to Calamity Brook's silvery white water rushing by under a footbridge. Calamity Brook derives its name from an incident that occurred in September, 1845, when Donald Henderson and others were searching for a more reliable water source for the MacIntyre Iron Works. As they prepared to camp for the night, Henderson threw his knapsack onto the ground. Unfortunately, it landed on a rock, causing a pistol he had packed inside to discharge accidentally and fatally wound Henderson. Falling to the ground, he looked up at his guide and said, "This is a hell of a place for a man to die." Ever since, the pond and brook have carried the name Calamity.

Despite its name, the rolling water of this brook is a blessing to me, such a simple and precious gift. I listen to the sounds, so soothing and peaceful, gracefully flowing over the river's rocks, carrying her spiritual gifts to all who will stop and listen along her journey to the Hudson and then on to the Atlantic Ocean.

Deep within, I believe that our real needs are satisfied in simple acts like this. Something in all of us wants to live a simpler lifestyle. We long for meaningful personal relationships, a sense of community, a sense of belonging. We want to feel that we make a difference to somebody, that what we are doing is valuable to the world. We do not want to leave this world without a trace of our existence, without loving and being loved. We do not want to be forgotten.

I've now set up camp for the night, having found a lovely, secluded spot in the Flowed Lands valley, still within ear-and-eye-contact of the Hudson. In a leisurely manner I unpack my gear and sort through the "kitchen cupboard" pocket of my backpack, looking for the "right" packet of dry food to transform into my evening meal. Boiling some water in my compact portable stove, I pour the contents of a macaroni and cheese envelope into a saucepan. Though hardly a gourmet delight, my simple supper seems to nourish more than my physical hunger.

Darkness is setting in as I finish cleaning up my cooking and eating utensils. Before I climb into my sleeping bag, I scribble some notes about the *soul things* that I've let slip away and now want to prioritize for my spiritual recovery.

Steps for a better quality of life might include:

◆ How can I better "Keep holy the Sabbath." Can I use Sundays in a way that leaves me feeling recreated and refreshed? Can I avoid using my Sabbath time for mall hopping or to catch up on work left over from the week?

◆ Similarly, can I follow Jesus' instructions to his disciples to come apart and rest awhile? Can I create mini-Sabbaths in the midst of my days and weeks to allow my soul and spirit to be nourished?

◆ Plan for some extended retreat time periodically in a quiet and prayerful setting — in the beauty of nature, if I can. Spend a little time meditating each day.

◆ Turn off the TV and the computer to spend more time with friends or to play outdoors.

◆ Rediscover those things that engender creativity and re-creation in my life. Take long awareness walks and let the senses absorb life around me.

These are not dramatic plans, but neither are they insignificant. These are some of the things that may again give me a pulse, a passion, a deep feeling for my life. If this list seems too long or difficult for you, maybe it can be reduced to the advice of the poet Kabir, who wrote: "Do you have a body? Don't sit on the porch! Go out and walk in the rain!" Such a simple step may begin a journey back to sensible and soulful living.

Gossamer Threads

Starting out on the hiking trails early in the morning, in the freshest part of the day, often produces the greatest clarity and insight. On this particularly cool morning that begins the second mile of my mountain retreat, moisture has condensed on the needles and leaves of the trees to give the forest a magical appearance. Sunlight illuminates grayish-blue bands of light slanted at diagonal angles that stretch between forest floor and treetops. The first one hiking the trail on mornings like this has the delightful experience of walking into the gossamer-like threads that some thoughtful spiders have spun across the trail during the night. For the hiker, they are only a slight annoyance and serve as a reminder that this is a shared habitat. These webs seem so insignificant, but they are an integral part of the spider's survival mechanism in the forest. There is nothing in our human engineering that can replicate these amazing threads. They can withstand strong winds, rain and vast temperature changes, and they can support much weight. NASA has not even comprehended anything with the size to weight strength ratio of these tiny webs. Observation tells me how swift and skillful these spiders are in making repairs or spinning new lifelines to the ones damaged by hikers like me.

These thin and seemingly insignificant threads teach me something about my daily life. Each day I make dozens of thread-like connections to others. The simple life rituals that I share with them — like meeting for coffee or lunch, taking a walk along a bike path, the smile or touch of a friend's hand, the laughter enjoyed in conversations about some silly thing like locking keys inside the car, hugs exchanged upon meeting or departing, a shared bike ride in the rain, a small adventure with children — all are moments that often go unnoticed or unappreciated. But, in the light of this early morning hike, I see how important such moments are in my daily life.

In these fleeting, transparent moments, someone is present listening to my dreams. Another is giving me inspiration or encouragement. A listening friend can diffuse my anger or frustration. As I hike today, I can recognize that these ordinary encounters are far from being trivial. Reflecting the spider's thin yet tenacious webs, these seemingly fragile threads of relationship are essential bonds of connection. They hold together a good part of my inner world and span my universe. They hold a meaning beyond my imagining.

Persons who minister to terminally ill patients underscore this point. They relate how often dying patients talk to loved ones about such ordinary moments. They don't waste precious time talking about their jobs or professional life. Dying patients never wish they had spent more time at the office; rather they regret not having carved out more time for fishing with their children or taking family vacations. Terminally ill patients often say how much they will miss sharing simple everyday moments of life with friends and family. Realizing now the brevity of life, they often try to mend relationships that have been broken due to misunderstandings, lack of sensitivity or neglect.

I once attended Dr. Ira Progoff's *Intensive Journal Workshop*. One of the exercises was to dialogue with persons who have been significant in our life story. These persons, some still living, some now deceased, have come into our lives and have had an impact on us for an entire lifetime. We were encouraged not to judge the content of these dialogues but rather to let the dialogue just flow as a stream of consciousness, as if that person were right in front of us.

As I scanned my life experiences for significant persons and began writing, I was amazed at how close to the surface my feelings about them were, even toward those far back in my life story. People like my second grade teacher, a childhood friend and a religious figure from the past started to emerge from lost memory, and I could see them in vivid detail just as I remembered them. My journaled conversations revealed to me how each of my influential persons is like a thread woven into the tapestry of my life story. Carrying their "presence" within me, I was surprised that I was putting into written form what I had never spoken to them aloud. I realized that some of the people who have meant the most to me have never heard me say "I love you" to them. I can't even remember telling my Dad I loved him until he was dying in Hospice. It took something that dramatic to break down the psychological barrier between these heartfelt feelings and my lips.

The workshop was insightful but scary. It challenged me to reveal emotions and feelings that were frozen within. It gave me an opportunity to thaw these feelings out and speak them. In its aftermath, perhaps I'll even begin to send flowers to loved ones while they are living rather than after they've died.

Wisdom people like Thich Nhat Hanh remind us to live each day "mindfully" and with full "awareness" of the moment. Scripture likewise reminds us to be vigilant: "Be on your guard, stay awake, because you never know when the time will come...stay awake, because you do not know when the master of the house is coming.... If he comes unexpectedly, he must not find you asleep. What I say to you I say to all: Stay awake!" (Mark 13: 33-37). Zen Buddhists talk about the transformation of our ordinary minds. How splendid it would be if we could wipe clean the slate of our minds each night and look at each new day with fresh wonder.

Such "seeing with new eyes" is a gift children offer to us. I think of how many times a child has made me stop and look at an insect, a flower, a bird. I cherish the times a child has helped me focus on the wonder in the world around me. Recently, I saw some children watching snow fall for the first time. It was a joyous moment for everyone present: the children, their parents, neighbors and other children. In *Prayers of a Thousand Years,* poet Coleman Barks tells a story that makes this point in a wonderful way:

> A child stood on his seat in a restaurant
> Holding the railing of the chairback
> As though to address a courtroom,
> "Nobody knows what's going to happen next."
> Then his turning-slide back down to his food,
> Relieved and proud to say the truth,
> As we were to hear it.

We certainly don't know what's going to happen next. The freshness of unfolding life is what makes each moment so important and unique. The ordinary can become very extraordinary when we see how fleeting it is and receive it as a gift. A shared life moment with those we love or revere makes an essential imprint in the deep places within our spiritual infrastructures.

Indeed, so often we fail to appreciate these vital connections until they are gone. Illness, death or moving away from family and friends awaken us to the real value of these gifts in our lives. Their absence is then felt as loss and sadness, and we begin to feel the ache of disconnection in our hearts. It's as if some "thief in the night" has come and stolen away our gift. In every funeral liturgy I preside at, I utter this prayer: "That we may come to understand ever more deeply the gift we are to each other in this life."

Having passed through the gossamer threads on my early morning hike, this leather tramp now begins to ascend Mount Marcy. As I make this transition on my morning trail, I am happy for the insights distilled from my pool of thoughts. And I want to make sure this "seeing" makes a transition into my everyday life. I don't want to be shocked into appreciation for what I have. In my daily conversations I often catch myself saying, "When I retire I will..." or, "Next year I will travel to...." The truth is, I have no guarantee about tomorrow. I receive my life breath-by-breath, moment-to-moment. I don't want to presume that I have a thousand tomorrows yet to live, that significant others will always be there in my life. I promise myself to become more pro-active about ordinary life moments and incidents, the essential webwork of my life.

Moving into the thicker woods along the mountain path, I'm presented with another image that illuminates these ordinary life moments. I'm drawn back to a religious experience I once had under a stand of giant Redwood trees in John Muir Woods in California. I remember looking upward through the canopy of those trees and feeling that my soul was ascending to an unbounded blue heaven. I was struck with awe by the majesty of these massive, ancient trees. I was surprised to learn that these trees, some of them thousands of years old and almost three hundred feet high, survive in part because of an almost unnoticed and subtle event that happens daily. Each morning, fog rolls in from the coast and condenses on the fine needles, forming dewdrops that fall to the ground supplying vital water to the trees. These giant trees have a very shallow and extensive root system that absorbs the drops and transports water to the top of the trees.

Who would have thought that the life of these

gigantic trees depends on such small, insignificant drops of water? Likewise, who among us would think that the delicate, web-like connections of our daily lives are responsible for so much unnoticed happiness and vitality?

Our casual encounters with friends, loved ones and the people we enjoy working with are our daily bread. While they may seem to pale in comparison to our mountain peak experiences, when we have eyes to see and hearts to understand, these gossamer bonds are like manna from heaven.

The petition in the Lord's Prayer, "Give us this day our daily bread," has taken on new meaning for me. It is more than a petition for the staple of food. It expresses my need for God to continue to feed me with the sustaining, nourishing presence of others in my life. Elijah's story from the Bible adds another dimension to the lesson of this second mile. In the First Book of Kings Elijah flees into a cave to save his own life and there encounters God. Yahweh tells him to:

> ...go out and stand on the mountain before Yahweh. Then Yahweh himself went by. There came a mighty wind, so strong it tore the mountains and shattered the rocks before Yahweh. But Yahweh was not in the wind. After the wind came an earthquake. But Yahweh was not in the earthquake. And after the earthquake came a fire. But Yahweh was not in the fire. And after the fire there came the sound of a gentle breeze. And when Elijah heard this, he covered his face with his cloak and went out and stood at the entrance of the cave. Then a voice came to him... (1Kings 19: 11-14).

Just as simply being present to each other in ordinary ways forms the fabric of meaning in our daily lives, precious life can be lost if we think that only the "big" events are important to us. Like Elijah, we can all realize that the ordinary, the quiet and the subtle can be epiphany moments of the divine presence in our lives.

The day is winding down on my second mile, so I set up camp and enjoy a light meal. As I savor both the food and today's hike, I am grateful to the spiders I never met who spun the gossamer webs along my path. Before the important life lessons they held vanish like a footprint on this trail, I write down some of my resolutions:

♦ To take more time to appreciate nature's microcosm, the often-unseen life-forms, sounds and patterns that create the fabric of our fragile existence.

♦ To cultivate and find concrete ways to express my gratitude to the special, interesting and wonderful people who walk with me on my life journey and whose presence brings joy.

♦ To spend more time with good friends and family and share meals with them. Reread Gospel stories of Jesus sharing meals with both friends and outcasts and notice the effects on those gathered around the table.

♦ To invite a group of friends over for simple celebrations at significant occasions, like having birthday desert to celebrate a friend's gift of life among us.

♦ To single out *soul friends* and spend a day together doing something fun.

♦ To again read *Anam Cara* by John O'Donohue with an eye to acquiring fresh insights on friendship.

♦ To send flowers to the living.

♦ To attend to the small, silent yet numinous moments that nourish the soul of my life fabric — and to make those moments times of prayer.

Mile Three

Wrestling with Your Angel

Jacob was left there alone. Then some man wrestled with him until the break of day. When the man saw that he could not prevail over him, he struck Jacob's hip at its socket, so that the hip socket was wrenched as they wrestled. The man said, "Let me go, for it is daybreak." But Jacob said, " I will not let you go until you bless me." "What is your name?" the man asked. He answered "Jacob." Then the man said, "You shall no longer be known as Jacob but as Israel because you have contended with divine and human beings" (Genesis 32: 25-31).

Trekking alone for long periods of time in the mountains can be a scary experience. I'm always alert to the possibility of stepping on an Eastern Timberback rattlesnake basking on a sunny ledge or of meeting a black bear lumbering toward me on the trail. However, these aren't the *scary* things that I'm concerned about as I begin this third mile of my trek. I'm less afraid of what might be peering at me from behind a tree or under a rock than of what's lurking within — my *shadow side*.

My shadow side might suddenly appear in my stream of consciousness as I hike these Adirondack mountain trails. When that happens, this peaceful forest can be changed into a wilderness of terror. I am alone with myself to face my demons. A wise person once said, "Wherever we go, we take ourselves along." Yet without the distractions of work or the demands of family life, we can become even more vulnerable to the shadow experience of our existence. Especially on a retreat or solitude experience, aspects of our personalities that have not yet been integrated might appear in many disguised ways. Ghosts from our past can have great negative power over us, disturbing our peace. Their surprise attacks can send us retreating in terror behind a safe emotional comfort zone of denial.

Current psychology would say that these are soul signs of our less-than-perfect self struggling for integration into our consciousness. We are, in a sense, twins. One aspect of us might portray ourselves as being calm, in control and having it all together. The other is the unredeemed side, the chaotic, confused and wounded self. This twin we usually hide out of sight from others.

These shadows may have had their source in the roles that society, our parents or other authority figures gave to us starting at the moment of our birth. They could be rooted in past childhood traumas in school, social or family life. These specters attempt to confine us within prisons of our own making. The echo of their voices can still be heard in the canyons of our memories: "What makes you think you can do that?" or "Just who do you think you are?" In the extreme, we might call ourselves "*racca*, fool." These inner voices from the past put us down and try to keep us chained to a dungeon wall of inferiority. They garb us with robes of inadequacy and poor self-worth. These shadows can easily paralyze our powers, sap our strength and stifle our creativity for a lifetime if we fail to wrestle with them. If repressed, they form holes in our souls, keeping us from becoming all we are intended to be in God's image.

In the marvelous *Earthsea Trilogy* by Ursula K. Le Guin, the main character, Sparrowhawk, is a wizard who is dogged by a demon shadow form. Sparrowhawk is always running away when this shadow bears down on him. He cannot perform his wizardry; he becomes vulnerable and weak. Finally, he stops running, does battles with this form and finally names the shadow. The demon doesn't vanish, but it no longer has power over him. The struggle enables Sparrowhawk to use his powers in full measure to do the good he desires to do.

Jim Whitaker, the famed climber of Mt. Everest, once said, "You never conquer the mountain. You only conquer yourself." As the stories of Sparrowhawk and the Biblical patriarch Jacob suggest, we may be wounded in the wrestling or unable to defeat our angels/demons. But when we engage our shadows rather than merely giving in, we access our birthright and our latent powers, and we move toward becoming whole. "Wholeness," adds Helen Luke, "is born of the acceptance of the conflict of human and divine in the individual psyche." As I climb this Adirondack trail, I reflect on how confronting our fears and shadows is truly to conquer an inner mountain.

Recently, I reread *The Spirituality of Imperfection* by Ernest Kurtz and Kathrine Ketcham. In the introduction they quote Francis T. Vincent, Jr., former Commissioner of Baseball:

> Baseball teaches us, or has taught most of us, how to deal with failure. We learn at a very young age that failure is the norm in baseball and, precisely because we have failed, we hold in high regard those who fail less often — those who hit safely in one out of three chances and become star players. I also find it fascinating that baseball, alone in sports, considers errors to be part of the game, part of its rigorous truth.

One of the salient points Kurtz and Ketcham make is that inner serenity and peace come from understanding and accepting our limitations and imperfections. "Rigorous truth" born out of humility teaches us that the threads of our past failures and pain can be woven together into a fabric of strength and growth for the future. Our failures can contribute to our personal sense of wisdom. It has taken me many years to get over a narrow understanding of the Gospel passage "Be perfect, as your heavenly Father is perfect" (Matthew 5: 48). Taking that passage out of context would lead to living out the myth of Sisyphus, condemned in our perfectionism to pushing a rock endlessly up a hill; the rock would always roll back before the task is accomplished. Looking at the rest of the Gospel message, however, would suggest replacing the word *perfect* with *compassionate*. Being compassionate as our heavenly Father is compassionate would give us a whole different spiritual orientation, one that calls us to more positive possibilities about ourselves. The simple and profound truth about ourselves is that we are not perfect, nor will we ever be. As Thomas Merton says, "We are a living incompleteness."

Sometimes in Scripture stories the demon is named before an exorcism occurs. Consider Jesus' forty days and nights in the desert, his time of deep inner struggle. Should he act like a wizard and change the stones to bread? Should he dazzle the crowds with spectacular feats, jump from the top of the temple and land unharmed? Should he be a political Messiah and conquer by military power? He is wrestling with his angel, even as Jacob did, questioning in what way God wants him to fulfill his mission. Some Scripture scholars suggest that this was not one incident that happened in the desert but, rather, was a constant discernment of purpose throughout Jesus' public life. Our demons will keep showing up. With Jesus and Jacob, we are in good company. Our task is to wrestle with our shadows, name them and thereby gain mastery over them.

As I hike over this mountain path, I reflect on how many wrestling matches of this kind I've had in the last twenty-five years of ministry. One particularly comes to mind. Seventeen years ago my niece Sara was born in Alaska. Two weeks after her birth my brother and sister-in-law flew down to the "lower 48" to celebrate her baptism. A good number of family members were at the airport to greet them upon arrival. I can remember the powerful loving feeling I experienced when I took their two-week-old baby in my arms. I had tears in my eyes as I held this fragile bundle of love. It must be something of what mothers or fathers experience with their first child. As a priest, I have held many babies at baptisms, home visits and other occasions. But this was different. I suddenly realized what I was giving up in accepting the vow of celibacy. I would never hold my *own* child. I would never be a father and have a parent-to-child relationship. I would not have a family. And now, this unexpressed part of myself was coming up to haunt me.

It appeared again when I was struggling with how I could continue to live in a structure so hierarchical and patriarchal. I was feeling strongly about the injustices within the Church's treatment of former priests and women religious and theologians who raised challenging questions. Inner shadows suggested that maybe it was time to experience the intimacy of a one-to-one relationship rather than the generic one-to-many model in congregational life. Some professionals might say I was in the throes of a mid-life crisis. I prefer to think of it as wrestling with my angel. In either case, there are times in our lives when the unexpressed side of ourselves jumps up and demands to be seen. We are given a glimpse of the road not taken. It's a time to reevaluate and choose another life path or to recommit to our original choice. If we choose to continue on the same path, it seems that it is necessary to deepen our commitment by recognizing deeper, more essential threads of our identity.

As I grappled with my angel, I sought out some

friends and my spiritual director to talk with. After some time I came to a realization that there is a difference between a *choice* and a *call*. Every day we make choices. Some, like whether or not to change jobs, are important in that they impact other big areas of our life. Others, like whether to do the grocery shopping today or tomorrow, are of no real consequence. Over my 28 years of ministry I have had to discern whether it is a life choice or is something I feel called to. My shadow was proposing a lifestyle that was very attractive, natural and good, but the problem was that I felt the call to continue ministry. In the tension of this crisis, I remember resisting, kicking against and being angry with God for this call. I felt certain that God would be OK with whatever decision I made. But I had to acknowledge that beneath that possible choice of another lifestyle was the haunting inner voice that my "living incompleteness" would become a kind of living unhappiness in the end.

In the midst of this wrestling match I became acutely aware that we can never really know God's will in most matters. As the Wisdom Scriptures say, "Who can know the mind of God?" (Wisdom 9:13). Yet one thing I learned from my spiritual director in discerning between a call and a choice is always to pray that you make the mistake God wants you to make. Ultimately, that kind of prayer is the only wrestling hold that has any real leverage.

As I make a turn on my mountain trail, I think of a friend of mine who recently had a severe wrestling match with his angel. For many years he had been struggling with his life issues. Like many of us in ministry, he was caught in a *virtue vice*. That's when we constantly live the appearance of being the perfect father, mother, wife, husband, minister or priest by always deferring our desires to the demands and needs of others. We ignore the needs of our own souls and our deep dreams and desires because we think that would be selfish. We are *supposed* to be selfless so that we can serve others *perfectly*. However, when the day comes that we can no longer live that way and we separate ourselves from our unreachable expectations, we walk into a storm. Mary Oliver describes this separation well in her poem "The Journey":

> One day you finally knew
> What you had to do, and began
> Though the voices around you
> Kept shouting
> Their bad advice—
> Though the whole house
> Began to tremble
> And you felt the old tug
> At your ankles.
> "Mend my life!"
> Each voice cried—
> But you didn't stay—
> You knew what you had to do...
> Little by little you left
> Their voices behind,
> Determined to save
> The only life you could save.

At different stages of our adult life we might suffer the anguish of our quintessential questions. Where is life for me? Is there any meaning in what I am doing for a living? Soon the wrestling match begins. Inevitably, those questions force us to face our inner truth. Poet David Whyte puts it this way: "You only have one life you can call your own, but there are a thousand others that you can call anything you want...it is better to try and fail than live someone else's life successfully."

Living someone else's life in place of your own is to forfeit the unique place created for you in the universe. Each of us is an original work of art; we each have a unique mission and purpose to fulfill. We may not see this divine design in our life, but it will unfold, like a flower that grows from seed.

A passage from the book of Jeremiah the Prophet (another figure who strongly resisted his call to ministry) offers encouragement. Jeremiah is told to go to the house of the Potter. There he watches clay being shaped by the patient hands of the Potter. If the vessel breaks or shapes badly, the Potter simply begins again. It is not discarded; it is refashioned. We should trust that the Divine Artist never grows weary of the task of shaping us into form. We will be shaped lovingly into the form that suits us best. Our flaws are worked into the finished form, weakness and strength fused together in balance. That is one of the beautiful things about being human: We are vessels of clay but carry a spark of the divine within. As Henry Nouwen suggested in his famous "wounded healer" concept, even our flaws can reveal our beauty. That is indeed what we are: wounded healers, flawed co-creators.

Maybe, like Michael Monohan, we need to forgive God for making us the way we are. In *Hearts on Fire* he prays:

> Lord, help me in my heart
> to forgive you
> for making me the way I am.
> Blasphemy? Perhaps.
> Honesty? For lack of a better word, yes...
> I have been told you made me
> Like yourself.
> Why then do we two
> Think so differently?
> You made me what I am, Lord.

Our struggles, our hearts' restlessness and our longing for some kind of radical fulfillment in life will, I am sure, keep us all on the mat with an angel from time to time. In the end, as we see in Jeremiah's story, God finds ways to "dupe" us, and we go on with our life. We pass through our struggles and, like Jacob in the morning, we part from our shadow and walk away with a limp.

Daylight is now ending on this third mile of my mountain retreat, and this leather tramp stops to make camp for the night. Preparing a quick supper of rice and beans, I light a candle and write down some points for further reflection:

♦ Meditate on Psalm 139: "O God, you search me and you know me...."

♦ Be aware of when I'm running from or suppressing my shadow — or from Psalm 139's "Hound of Heaven" — and be more ready to wrestle.

♦ When trekking through the scary stretches of this life journey, remember to breathe deeply and trust the Divine Potter.

♦ Write prayers forgiving God and myself for not being perfect.

♦ Read once again *The Spirituality of Imperfection*.

♦ List three endearing qualities that I have in my personality for every flaw I perceive.

♦ Write a paragraph about five things I really feel good about having done in my life.

♦ Trace back to the sources those voices that have depreciated or defeated me. Then, name them and release them.

♦ It is always worth talking over major decisions with a wise friend.

♦ Remember: "To thine own self be true."

Mile Four

The Accident of Birth

As I break camp and prepare to begin the fourth mile of my hike, I reflect on how this kind of trekking is high on physical demand and low on creature comforts. A swim in a cold lake replaces a hot shower, a seat made of sod replaces a sofa, and one does not change clothes every day. However, as I gather my gear, I'm well aware that I do hike in some comfort. I am equipped with a pair of Vasque sundowner leather Gore-Tex boots and a state-of-the-art Lowe backpack. I can layer my clothing to match weather conditions. I carry a wide assortment of dry foods to cook.

I can remember back to the late 50s, when I first began camping and backpacking. Camping equipment was purchased from a local army/navy store. We all looked like we were someplace in between the boy scouts and the army. Tents and packs were made with lots of heavy canvass. Hiking boots were standard non-waterproof work shoes of the day. Over time, improvements were gradually introduced, like boots with steel-tip toes. How things have changed! Gone are the days of bedrolls and birch bark shelters. By the late 60s A-frame tents and external aluminum framed packs appeared, and nylon clothing replaced wool pants and the classic checkered lumberjack shirts. L.L. Bean 60/40 windbreaker parkas could be sighted everywhere in the woods. Mummy bags of down were carried instead of blankets. Hiking boots were constructed of fabric and leather and didn't require a lifetime to break in. I remember my lightweight Swedish-built Siva stove that would burn several kinds of fuel, including good whiskey — although I never heard of anyone sacrificing any for that purpose.

A 1983 *Business Week* article showed the direction in which backpacking had moved. Affluent readers were advised that a complete outfit for camping required an initial outlay of $750-$1,250, but that this investment was prudent because it "is so sturdy and normally used only three or four times a year." In other words, many campers of the 1980s became (a) well-heeled; (b) quipped with an array of state-of-the-art gear and (c) expected to dabble in the activity for only a few days per year. Nobody was packing in the old heavy black skillets or the famed Hudson Bay ax, affectionately called the "shin splitter" since swinging its truncated handle downward put your shins in jeopardy if you happened to miss the log. Swiss army knives were simple and replaced the larger "bear stabbers" that were worn on the belt in Jim Bowie fashion.

The image of a woodsman standing around wearing an old worn plaid shirt with suspenders and smoking a pipe changed as well. David Brooks' article "Cell Phone Naturalists" from a recent issue of *The Utne Reader* captures the change eloquently: "For the true nature techies, some things, like boots and sport-utility vehicles, should be as big as possible. Other things, like stoves and food packs, should be as small as possible.... In the 70s the polyester people were low-class disco denizens, now they are high-status environmentalists." Brooks' favorite item is a Titanium OmniTech parka with double-ripstop nylon, supplemented with ceramic particles and waterproof taped seams: "Here I am in the middle of the forest and I'm wearing *Starship Enterprise.*" Some hikers now carry cell-phones and GPS systems in case someone wants to know just where in the world they happen to be.

While I am contemplating all of this, a disconcerting contrasting image comes to my mind. Suddenly, I am transported with all my gear and placed among refugees returning to Guatemala from Mexico. I am now walking with them in memory as I once did in reality through the highlands of Guatemala. They are carrying pieces of tin that will serve as a roof for the night. Their possessions include gourds of water and small sacks of corn and beans. They travel barefoot, without comfort or safety, in the dense forest. In an age when we are obsessed with the speed and memory capacity of our computers, these refugees have yet to make their first phone call. The cost of my hiking clothing and gear is probably more than they earn in twelve months.

Even as I hike on, I'm weighed down by the sad fact that refugees are growing in number across our globe. They total over 23 million, displaced from land and homes by civil war, famine or ecological disaster. Consider the recent plight of ethnic Albanians in Kosovo living in terror of Serb soldiers as they faced the winter without food, shelter and heat.

I also think about the historical predicament of Native Americans as I walk through these deep woods that once were their hunting grounds. Perhaps the most striking example is the infamous *Trail of Tears,* when the people of the Cherokee Nation were forced to march from the eastern United States to the Indian Territory in Oklahoma. That long journey, filled with suffering and the most extreme hardship, caused the death of tens of thousands of American Indians.

A U.N. report states that more than two and a half billion people live on only two dollars a day. There isn't one item in my pack that cost less than two dollars. It further says that the combined wealth of the world's richest 225 people is the same as the income of the rest of the world's 2.5 billion people.

The plight of our planet's desperate people comes into our comfortable homes nightly on the news. They can't see us, and we would prefer not to see them.

Their suffering and our comfort seem so incompatible. We feel overwhelmed by so large a scale of human misery that we suffer from compassion fatigue.

As human beings we all have the same basic needs: food, water, clothing, a safe place to live, meaningful work to sustain daily life. We seek love and support from family and community. Though our skin color and customs may differ, we are basically and humanly all the same. We carry the same essential needs and yearnings of the heart. A smile and a tear are understood in any language.

The only difference among us is the *accident of birth*. Why was I born here, not there? Why am I living in comfort and in a place that is relatively free from the effects of war, while millions are threatened daily by violence or natural disasters? As I walk along today's mountain path, I review all the material advantages that I enjoy and too often take for granted, like my blessings of health, food and shelter. I have the benefit of an education and profession that give me social mobility and prestige. All these circumstances force me to face the question of how to use my learning, money and time for the good of others. Indeed, how can I stand comfortably on an island of affluence while billions of my fellow human beings are drowning in a sea of misery?

I have been carrying these thoughts for some distance, and they are far heavier than all the gear in my high-tech backpack. I could let myself feel overwhelmed, but, instead, a small spark of hope flashes another insight before me: *the power of things small*. I recall a story in the New Testament about faith "the size of a mustard seed" that can move mountains (See Luke 13: 18-19). I don't have to have extraordinary faith; just a small measure is enough to start something. I think of the force of the lowly widow against the unjust judge who finally renders a decision in her favor because she is persistent (See Luke 18: 1-8). This is an especially strong example since in that culture she would have typically needed a male family member to advocate her cause. As a woman, she had no power.

Yet there is infinite power in small things. The human egg cell that produced a Jesus, a Buddha or a Gandhi, weighs only about one twenty-millionth of an ounce. In each case, however, a microscopic beginning changed the very face of the earth.

Jesus tells the story of how a small measure of leaven mixed into the bread causes the whole loaf to rise (See Luke 18: 20-21). In the same way, just a few concerned individuals can be agents of change in a society. The witness of Fr. Roy Bourgeois and a handful of others (fewer than fifty) began a prophetic movement in the early 90s to close the School of the Americas at Fort Benning, Georgia, where the U.S. Army trains Latin American soldiers in techniques of terror. Just a few years later, more than ten thousand would gather each year to protest the evil this institution perpetrates on poor indigenous peoples in Latin America. Bourgeois and others have served much prison time for their protest.

Look also at the humble beginnings of the nonviolent movements led by Mahatma Gandhi against the mighty British Empire, or of Nelson Mandela against the deeply entrenched system of apartheid in South Africa, or of Martin Luther King, Jr. against the cultural patterns of prejudice in America. In each case, the leaven of liberation and justice arose out of a pinch of faith and promise. Indeed, throughout history many social changes have occurred because small groups have banded together for a just cause.

The Gospel story of the loaves and fishes generates further encouragement that wondrous things can happen even when we start with limited resources. The multitude of five thousand has been following Jesus. Now they are in a deserted spot. The disciples tell Jesus that the crowd is not only hungry for his words, but now at day's end they are hungry for bread as well. "You give them something to eat" (Mark 6: 37), Jesus tells them. Yet how can they do that with just five loaves and a couple of fish? Before we know it, however, the limitations have been changed into a miracle of abundance. What a picnic! All are fed, and there are baskets of food left over.

Some theologians suggest that the real miracle was that the crowd learned from the example of the boy who offered what little he had. Influenced by the leaven of his act, the rest of the multitude began to share with each other. Smallness and the feeling of powerlessness when combined with a measure of faith can be a powerful force for good.

The Quakers use the expression, "Speak the truth to power." If I see a wrong and do not make it known to those in power, then I am guilty. But if I speak the truth to power and they fail to act, then they are responsible for the evil. I think of Dorothy Day, co-founder of the Catholic Worker movement, confronting the powerful Cardinal Spellman of New York about the evil of militarism in our country. She was a pebble that stood against a mountain of power. Yet her witness moved the mountain. In time her position was acknowledged and incorporated into a wise and influential document on peace written by the U.S. Catholic Bishops.

Simple acts like writing a letter to the editor or to an elected official are other ways of speaking the truth to power. Amnesty International, one of the world's preeminent human rights groups, encourages its members to write letters to oppressive governments to free "prisoners of conscience." The result has been the saving of prisoners' lives in both East and West. Thousands of letters raining down on government officials are like drops of water that eventually wear down a rock. Testimony from released prisoners brings tears to one's eyes and attests to the effectiveness of this practice of letter writing. It's amazing to think that something as simple as writing a letter can save a life. The point is that the effect of small actions multiplies our individual efforts, and we come to sense our solidarity with a multitude of like-minded persons.

People are effecting such change in the social order all over the earth: in China, in Peru, in Brazil, in the United States. These efforts are fueled by faith and by creative imagining. Each of us can envision possibilities of justice and peace. Nor should we put limits on what such creative imagination might lead to.

The important thing is to begin by doing something, no matter how small it seems. In the words of a popular saying: "I cannot do everything, but I can do something." A small action is the first step that breaks the paralysis of inaction and the feeling of hopelessness. Volunteering to serve others at a homeless shelter or in a neighborhood fix-up, working at a food bank, tutoring a student in math, joining an environmental action group, getting involved in the political process as an informed and active voter — these are small but important ways to give something back.

My action may not realign the world's wealth, but it makes me all the richer for giving. And I believe that the circle of compassion will ever widen to where there is need. One of anthropologist Margaret Meade's famous quotes is: "Never doubt that a small group of thoughtful citizens can change the world: indeed it's the only thing that ever has."

Wendell Berry adds:

> Every day do something
> that won't compute. Love the Lord.

Love the world. Work for nothing...
Ask the questions that have no answers.
Invest in the millennium. Plant sequoias.

As I set up camp for the night, I am still finding the accident of my birth to be quite an enigma. I need to reflect on how to address the inequality of this accident in my work-a-day world after I return from this trek. I want to seek concrete ways to live in solidarity with people who are doing little thing for others.

Simply put, I want to further explore how I can give something back, how can I serve the needs of others whose birth situation was just different from mine. Some points that I would like to ponder:

♦ How can I increase my awareness of those in need around the world? Can I lessen my need to anesthetize or armor myself in the face of the constant media coverage of injustice and tragedies around our globe?

♦ What kind of prayerful solidarity with the poor and needy can redress compassion fatigue?

♦ How can I learn more about organizations that are really serving the needs of less-advantaged human beings?

♦ Is it possible to tithe my money and time, volunteering with an organization that has direct hands-on contact with those in need?

♦ Knowing it can be an effective practice, why not make time to write letters to the editor and elected representatives urging support for policies and laws that benefit poorer people at home and abroad?

♦ Can I not learn more about other cultures and peoples by going on travel seminars and retreats with organizations that sponsor such trips?

The insight of today's fourth mile of my mountain retreat seems significant in addressing the quintessential questions of my life journey. The inner gesture of extending my awareness and compassion toward those born in less fortunate situations than mine seems to put my own questions and my quest for meaning into a balanced perspective. As I zip up my down sleeping bag for the night, I sigh a prayer of gratitude for the blessings of today's hike, and for the accident of my birth as well.

Mile Five

Canada Geese

An early start on the trail this morning put me under the faint but familiar "honking" of migrating Canada Geese, one of the most widely distributed water birds of North America. Some have a wingspan of more than 6 feet, an impressive sight, especially in the clarity of the mountain horizon. I stop at an open space on this rocky, root-exposed trail and scan the sky for their unmistakable signature, that beautiful ribbon-like flying "V" or echelon formation.

These birds are true migrators, unlike sub-species that stay in the Northeast all winter foraging around the ponds of golf courses and suburban apartment complexes. Migrating birds have been a source of wonder for centuries. What mechanism suddenly trips off and causes them to "lift off"? (In the case of Canada Geese, the female lifts off first, followed by the male.) What causes them to migrate from hundreds of lakes and ponds in the north and make this annual trip to their feeding grounds in the south? What guidance system puts them on the exact same flyways that their ancestors took eons before?

The mystery of migration is a seasonal phenomenon for many birds (and also for insects like the Monarch Butterfly). They use landmarks and even stars to guide them to their destination. Some think that these creatures use the sun since it always points south at noon, allowing migrating birds to calculate their direction based on their internal 'clock' and the sun's position at mid-day. These birds are said to be sensitive to polarized light and ultraviolet light, which are expressed differently depending on the position of the sun. In cloudy weather Canada

Geese require only a small opening in the clouds to read the sun's guiding rays. Some research on birds says that, like the Monarch, they use a magnetic field to navigate.

Flying is the most strenuous form of locomotion in the animal world, but also the most direct. These migratory creatures leave Canada and fly thousands of miles south to Chesapeake Bay. Their fly route is passed on from generation to generation, parent geese teaching their children. The leader is the first to break the air resistance of flight. Each bird in the formation creates an uplift of air currents that helps to lift the one behind. By flying in a "V" formation, the whole flock has 70% greater flying range than if each bird flew alone.

As I look overhead on this morning trek, I count more than one hundred of these black-silhouetted winged forms gracefully moving against a deep blue sky. The sun reflects a silver-like shadow on the underside of their large wings, making it seem as though they are sending coded farewell messages to viewers standing below.

We seldom think of animal species as living in community, but these geese exhibit a high degree of interdependence every mile of their common journey. Canada Geese mate for life and are very protective of their partners. When a goose gets sick, wounded or shot down, two other geese drop out of formation and follow it down to help and protect it. They stay with it until it dies or is able to fly again. Then, together they launch out with another formation or catch up with the flock.

What an example of loyalty and fidelity they model to us for our relationships. Like these geese, we are all interdependent. Whether we are a community of two, twenty-two or two hundred, we are helped and made stronger by each other's encouragement and support. This is the gift of community. I have to ask myself if I have been there for my friends and family in their time of need as these geese are to each other.

Theirs is a dangerous migratory trip. They fly thousands of miles through changing weather patterns. They face the threat of seasonal hunters aiming their guns at them the entire distance. It's made more difficult because of the vast destruction of their wetland habitat. But, through it all, they stay together as a community. What a wonderful message they give us in our sometimes-perilous journey of life: Stay together! Help each other get through challenging times.

In my busy life in the city I have seen this spectacular sky show many times, but I'm usually in too much of a hurry to give it my full attention. I don't stop and appreciate the miracle of these wonderful fly-overs. Here in the mountains, however, it's different. Without the rush of traffic, the din of city noise or a too-full agenda, I can just stop and lean against this giant steel-gray erratic (a boulder left behind by a retreating glacier) and watch this spectacle as if time or schedules don't exist.

These majestic creatures are among the few remaining large bird species that dot our skies each migrating season. Sadly, many others have vanished from sight. I can only imagine what it must have felt like when the sky was filled with clouds of large flocks of migrating birds making their way south in the autumn. They would also be the first harbingers of spring upon their return north. For me, regardless of the time of year, their presence signals a hope-filled new season of life.

Here in the mountains I sense that our earthen home is a shared habitat and that our lives and destinies are somehow interrelated with all other living species. As I watch the "V" vanish in the distance, I look on these creatures with a renewed sense of respect and awe. A stirring breeze nudges me to move on. I lift my backpack from the damp forest floor, and with the sun in my face I begin my trek again, carrying grateful insights of life gained from this brief and fleeting experience.

Having watched the geese fly south, I think about my own internal guidance system. Sometimes, I feel an internal *click* that starts calling me to change directions, to pack it in and move on. I begin scanning the horizons of my choices. I can't explain what causes this *trip off* except to say that maybe it is a change of seasons in my life. In the midst of my present unsettledness and searching I wonder if a divine wisdom is at work guiding both these migrating geese and the change in my life direction. The Creator has placed within both me and the geese a device for survival. In me, it directs a search for meaning so necessary for my soul's survival. In the geese it's survival on a natural level, expressed in escape to a warmer climate. Are not both quests under a loving providence?

I believe that when these internal feelings to move on begin to stir within me, a door of opportunity correspondingly opens, if the stirrings are from the Spirit of God. It is my belief that the Divine Power who put a "migratory response" in birds and insects and who provides for them wintering grounds to fly to would act as graciously for me. Would this Divine Power who shapes my life not provide me with inner resources to address the deep unsettled feelings that are part of the fabric of my being? I would like to believe that a divine providence is giving me wings to take me where I am supposed to be. At the deepest level I have a sense of destiny and purpose and mission. Like the hidden underside of a tapestry, I can't always see how all the threads are tied together to make up the picture on the other side. Yet I trust that I am important enough to be watched over and guided by a loving Creator.

"To the Waterfowl," a poem by William Cullen Bryant comes to mind:

He, who, from zone to zone,
Guides through the boundless sky thy certain flight,

In the long way that I must tread alone,
Will lead my steps aright.

In these majestic mountains I sense deeply that a loving God is at work guiding both our universe and my personal life, that this vast universe is animated by providence and wisdom.

I remember my early years in ministry when I would worry about the impact I was making in the lives of people who came to me for guidance or spiritual direction. I worried about my effect on their relationships with each other and with God. Then while on a retreat in a monastery I asked the Abbot for advice. He listened patiently for more than a half-hour and then said, "Rich, the Spirit of God has been moving over the waters of chaos since the beginning of time. The little bit of confusion that you might create by your choices and decisions won't throw God." His words helped me realize that God is really in charge, not me. Immediately, I felt free. The torturous cage of introspection had been opened, and I flew to freedom. From this perspective I could take risks and laugh at my mistakes, believing that even they could be carriers of God's grace. While not taking my work casually, gone were my worry years.

I may never fully know if the choice I am making at any given time is the right one — or if it is God's will. I can only pray that I make the mistake that God wants me to make. The prayer of Thomas Merton is a spiritual gem to remember and pray in times of transition:

My Lord God, I have no idea where I am going.
I don't see the road ahead of me.
I cannot know for certain where it will end.
Nor do I really know myself....
And the fact that I think I am following your will
Does not mean that I am actually doing it.
But I firmly believe that the desire to please you
Does in fact please you.

And I hope I have that desire in all that I am doing.
I hope that I will never do anything apart from that desire.
And I know that if I do this, you will lead me by the
    right road,
Though I know nothing about it.
Therefore, I will trust you always,
Though I may seem to be lost and in the shadow of death.
I will not fear, for you are ever with me and you will
Never leave me to face my perils alone.

Amen, Amen, Amen.

Like the Canada Geese, we look for signs all along the flyways of our journeying. There will be times when we might feel that it's a big sky and we are so small, that the distance is too great and the headwinds too strong. It is then that we need to draw strength from the belief that we are not alone in our discernment. Providential love will prevail.

I've reached trail's end for the fifth day of my mountain retreat. An open space of meadow and a silent standing Adirondack lean-to will be home for me tonight. As I approach the lean-to, I notice all the carved initials on the floor and the log beams, reminders of others who over the years have trekked ahead of me in this wilderness. I glug down some water to slake my thirst and sit with my back against the old log wall of the lean-to, quietly absorbing the sight of fading goldenrod and the sound of crickets hidden in the grass. It is a place beautifully rich with God's gifts.

I intend to make a mental review of today's insights and questions. Like jewels, I will hold them up to the light of reflection, hoping I might glean some precious answers for my quintessential questioning. Perhaps some wisdom will shine on my life experience through the prism of this fifth mile of my trek to teach me something new. But first, I prepare to celebrate a simple supper.

I paw my way into my propped-up backpack,

searching for my food cache of easy-cook spaghetti. The stove cooperates and contributes its hot blue flame under the pot of water that looks like it needs some serious boiling. As I lean back against the wooden frame again, I can feel my tired back muscles beginning to relax, relieved of the load I've carried here. Taking off my hiking boots and stretching out my legs over the wooden floor, I let the stove take over the work now. It feels so good to be here. While waiting for the water to boil, I find myself thinking about what I learned on the trail today. I take out my leather tramp journal and start to sift through and record some of those insights for further development later tonight.

I begin my musings with a paradox. Here, as I hike, eat and reflect in solitude, I come to an ever deeper appreciation of the value and importance of community. It is seemingly contradictory that withdrawing from others has enhanced my appreciation for companionship.

Secondly, I realize that it is always good to unpack our stuff with someone who is wise and who can *really* listen. Sometimes just talking it out will help us unload the emotional weight pressing upon us. The best listening friends are the ones who don't feel they have to give us answers; they simply listen. Remember the Biblical character Job? His friends listened to his laments, and, in fact, they added to his torment with their "answers." Most of us, however, have one or two good listening friends we can seek out to share our inner thoughts with as we travel along our life journey.

My third insight is to lighten up and laugh a lot more. I shouldn't take myself so seriously. I am not in charge of the universe. Laughter can give perspective. It's a lever to free us from ego-imprisonment. When I feel my ego is overly involved in my decisions, I lose my freedom to be indifferent to the results. A sense of humor not only reduces up-tightness and stress, it also makes what I do more effective.

Another lesson learned from the Canada Geese is that we need to be present to each other — in the good and bad times. Canada Geese make it through their arduous journey as a tightly knit community. Sharing our feelings and concerns with our companions, listening to their counsel and drawing strength from their love can serve to keep us on a straighter life course. The word companion is a combination of two Latin words: *con*, which means "with," and *panus*, which means "bread." A companion is, thus, someone we break bread with. What a wonderful word! Our companions are with us for the soul-sharing needs we carry within. They are the ones who listen to our stories but don't overwhelm us with their advice.

Chief Linchwe II, head of the Bakgatla tribe and one of the founders of Botswana, tells a story of two men, one blind and the other unable to walk. So the two decided to work together. The blind man carried the crippled man on his back. One had the feet; the other had the eyes. One day, they met a lion. In his fright the blind man threw the crippled man down and ran away. The lion, of course, killed the crippled man because he could not run and then the blind man because he could not tell where he was going. Both died because both had lost sight of the fact that their lives in this world were necessarily bound up with each other.

Pondering this story, I realize what my life might be like without these gifts of community and companionship. Like the Canada Geese, our true friends stay with us through it all. They tend to our wounds when we are depressed or frustrated by failures, and they deepen our good times and achievements. They keep vigil with us in the dark nights of the soul and keep us on course when the journey seems smooth. They break through the walls of isolation we tend to build around ourselves in our times of need, and they multiply our joy in our times of celebration. They provide soul power for our lives, and their caring teaches us to be gentle with ourselves in all our life circumstances. If we try to "tough it out" in life as rugged individualists, we not only miss out on one of life's greatest gifts and leave undeveloped one of our greatest human potentials, we risk ultimate failure in our life journey.

As I clean up my gear after my evening meal, I reflect on how sighting the Canada Geese truly gave me a lift today. I don't feel so alone or lost in this big world. I have more positive feelings of trust in divine providence in my life. I know I have good friends for support in times of transition or risk-taking. I am more confident that somehow all will be well as I move forward in my life direction. I feel that my little life plan somehow fits into the larger plan of Providence. I can believe that a door of opportunity will open when I choose to answer the call to do something different with my life. Finally, today's reflections lead me to make these resolutions:

♦ Review times in my life when even seemingly bad choices or failures later had good consequences.

♦ Develop a trust that *all* my life experiences contribute to my personal wisdom about life.

♦ Meditate on the passages of Scripture that deepen a sense of trust in divine providence.
  ⇨ Isaiah 43: 18-19 ("I am doing something new.")
  ⇨ Jeremiah 29: 11-14 ("I have plans in mind for you.")
  ⇨ Luke 11: 1-13 ("Seek and you will find.")
  ⇨ Matthew 6: 25-34 ("Do not worry about your life.")

♦ Ponder what I have learned about the meaning of the words *companion* and *friend.*

♦ Consider the lilies of the field.

Mile Six

Starry Night Sky

After another full day of backpacking, and having reached my desired destination, I set my gear up in a lean-to near the Opalescent River. I've been listening to her lyrical voice the last two miles inviting me to stay for the night. I roll out my well-compressed sleeping bag over the wide, sandy, worn plank floor. I strike a wooden match to fire up the cookstove, and gray-blue smoke begins to penetrate my nostrils, causing a brief coughing spell. It doesn't, however, deter my getting ready for a meal of vegetable lasagna (cooked in an envelope rather than an Italian kitchen) and for an evening of relaxation. The flame on the stove kicks in, and I fine-tune it too a light blue streak. It triggers my anticipation and excitement about the spectacular treat that will crown this sixth mile of my mountain retreat: the starry night sky.

When darkness comes, I look for the largest open space of sky that will allow me to view the vastness of the star-filled heavens above. In these remote mountains free of light pollution, the night sky is transparently displayed in all her mysterious grandeur. In the silent and gentle transition from daylight to night, I reflect on how for those of us living in the Western Hemisphere this day is ending, while for people in the Eastern Hemisphere a new day is dawning. As I pray in wordless gratitude for this day I have lived, someone there is offering a prayer of appreciation for the gift of a fresh day of life.

I have often noticed that whenever people stand under the starry dome of heaven and look up at the moon or planets, the usual response is one of silent awe. As Bishop Robert Morneau poetically suggests:

> All of us stutter and stumble in the presence of
> a sunset, a friendship, a star. Such is life.

Why are we fascinated with space? Could it be because of some kind of genetic memory hidden deep within our DNA, a recalling of our cosmic origins in the big bang?

Our ancient ancestors who lived outdoors under heaven's dome were true contemplatives. (This word, taken from the Latin, *con* and *templum*, means being one with the temple.) They gave names to the constellations and told the stories of their origins. The myths told by hunter-gatherers encircling a fire at night under the stars or by shepherds on hillsides are still a source of fascination for us. They speak of the human love, envy, jealousy, power and playfulness played out in the constellations. Sailors at sea stood night watch reading the star-filled sky as a map to their destination and at times divined their destiny there as well. Our ancestors studied the order, harmony and beauty of the domed temple of the sky. Their dream was to create here on earth what they observed in the heavens. The night sky above my mountain campsite likewise wraps me in its cloak of mystery, restoring a primitive reality in my soul.

My favorite position for viewing the stars is lying on my back looking up from the earth. It lets me contemplatively take in the spacious nighttime majesty. Surrounded by mountains and trees, this evening's view of the big sky is somewhat limited, but I can still see a sizeable opening of sky above. Settled in my closed cell mattress pad, my eyes begin to adjust. Silently, I let the heavens cover me with darkness and mystery in what I call my *soul-to-sky* connection. The twin sisters of *solitude* and *silence* are seductively present in this dark landscape. Wordlessly they lead me into the heavenly chambers, and I am rapt in their charmed presence. Enveloped in the dark, I sense that I am in the presence of something sacred.

Mystics have attempted to express this experience in what is called the *apophatic* tradition (from the Greek *apophasis*, which means denial or negation) or the *via negativa*. From this perspective, God is held to be "apophatic" or beyond our human comprehension. We can speak of God only by using negatives. God is not this, not that, not anything we can know or understand. Ultimately, we are reduced to silence before such mystery. We enter what St. John of the Cross described as the dark night of the soul. While the *kataphatic* tradition, the *via positiva* or the way of light, says that we arrive at an understanding of God by affirming creation as a reflection of God, Christian mystics such as John and Meister Eckhart suggest that God is to be known in a kind of *unknowing*. This *via negativa* is summed up in the title of the famous 14th century text, *The Cloud of Unknowing* and in the Zen notion, the "emptiness of fullness."

So often in Scripture darkness is associated with sin and evil. But it also includes a sense of the *holy dark* that we see in the silence of Jesus' quiet prayer times or in the sacred empty space out of which creation first emerged. To appreciate the positive side of the dark, we need only consider the darkness of the womb, which is something wonderfully creative and mysteriously life-giving. And the darkness of the Advent season is a time of joyful expectation as we await the birth of the Son of Justice. The darkness of a night sky can likewise convey a sense of *mystery*, *spaciousness* and *profound life* in a very powerful way.

I hear a small chorus of crickets in the distant darkness as stars of different magnitude begin to sparkle like diamonds set in the black velvet above. These heavenly luminaries have a unique beauty not captured by any form of neon light.

Rabbi Abraham Heschel, a Jewish theologian and mystic, prayed, "I did not ask for success; I asked for wonder. And you gave it to me." Heschel had a sense of "the holy dimension of existence." He saw wonder and awe as gifts that precede faith. A star-filled night sky is truly a religious experience, a source of wonder, awe and joy. Sometimes we allow our daily life to become jaded, drained of wonder. We need exposure to something so big that we cannot help but be overwhelmed by life's vastness and beauty. The starry sky is one such gift that is always available. Observing the spaciousness of the cosmos, one feels transported to the edge of eternity.

I recall one spectacular summer night when a group of us were on a canoe trip in Nova Scotia. We had paddled for two days to Frozen Ocean Lake deep into the interior of the rugged Canadian province. The place was so desolate that we didn't encounter another person during our whole time there. As remote and isolated as the area was, it paradoxically provided an ideal environment for a larger intimacy.

The first night, long enough after sunset for our eyes to be accustomed to the darkness, we sat quietly at the edge of the lake. Our home galaxy, the Milky Way, became present to us with amazing clarity and directness. It was so thick with the commingling of stars in every direction that it would take an eternity to number them. For earth is two-thirds of the way from the center of this galactic miracle, and our small planet floats in this great body of the Milky Way. Moreover, our galaxy floats within an immensely larger universe of over two billion still-unexplored galaxies.

The sparkling heavenly display of this jeweled universe dazzled our imagination and reduced us all to total silence. Our inner reality was reflected in the absolute stillness of the night; there wasn't even a hint of a breeze. All the stars of the Milky Way above were mirrored on the perfectly calm lake so that we felt suspended between two heavens. We got into our canoes and gently launched out onto the surface of the water, gliding through a sea of stars. It felt like cruising on a timeless space odyssey. When we came to a stop out in the shimmering lake, we lay down in our canoes and just floated beneath the luminous vault of heaven above, absorbed in the infinite chasm of space.

As I now lie here in the Adirondacks, beneath that same magnificent night show, it occurs to me that each point of starlight is visible due to the dark space surrounding it. It is because of being framed in darkness that each star shines in its unique beauty. Even "clustered" stars like the *Pleiades* are distinguished from each other by the open spaces between them. If it weren't for the darkness, we would never see these points of light.

Several lessons emerge for me in this observation. My first awareness is that in the vastness of this universe there is such beauty and harmony that even the smallest element has infinite value. Within these billions of galaxies, each one of us is a unique creature. Each of us has a one-of-a-kind genetic package of DNA; there are no carbon copies. Each of us was "loved into existence" by a Divine Lover and given a unique role in the story of the universe. The awareness that the story is more complete because of my existence in it gives me a deep sense of my personal value. More clearly than ever, I feel that I don't have to prove my worth. I am important for no other reason than the fact that I exist.

Moreover, the darkness, stillness and clarity of the nighttime sky give me the inner spaciousness to appreciate my inherent value. Contemporary life is often too cluttered to allow for such spacious awareness. We have lost the natural balance between day and night present in aboriginal cultures. Their life rhythm provided space between work and rest. The night was a time for rest and sleep to restore strength used during the day's labor. Our technological society has extended the daylight hours with electricity, allowing us to substitute the natural rest rhythm with more work far into the night. While many of us now lack sleep, there is no shortage of research and articles on the topic of the "Overworked American."

As I lie here peacefully on the forest floor looking at the stars after a day of arduous hiking, I wonder why I am becoming such a workaholic. Even at this moment, as I savor and find rest in the dark areas of the night sky, I'm aware that the more carefully I look for the *space between* the stars, the more *stars* I see! My life is like that: My times of rest often only bring into focus all the things that need to be done. Now, most of that activity is worthwhile and even wonderfully bright and star-like. Yet if I don't intentionally keep a balance, my daily schedule gets filled with too many things to do. My task lists become like hurdles on a track, and I feel I must get over them as fast as possible so I can reach the finish line. Too often I end the day tired, with little energy left for reading, writing, working on a hobby or taking a walk. Similarly, not leaving enough space between my work and play impacts both negatively. It then feels like I have to work hard even at playing.

Anthropologist Michael Harner writes about "soul loss," which happens to us as we lose touch with the natural world around us. In contemporary North American Hispanic communities, soul loss is called *susto* and is considered a common condition in the modern world.

The healing and reversal of soul loss takes place in the forest at night, as the person is returned for a while to the land he or she once knew. Such people are often cured through their renewed connections, their visions of animals, snakes and plants. The cure for soul sickness is not in books. It is written in the bark of a tree, in the moonlit silence of night, in the bank of a river and the water's motion.

Harner's notion offers us an alternative to couch therapy. The experience of wilderness solitude and a sense of spaciousness in the mountains can cure soul loss and race the pulse of our spirituality again. The calm, peacefulness and the beauty of what we experience in its creative space can fill our hearts and flow into our daily living. Such therapeutic practices as cultivating a sacred experience under the temple of the heavens can deepen our contemplative side. These simple activities can put us in touch with new and refreshing sources of spirituality for our lives. Look upward into the sky night and day; in each season of change there will be signs of hope to inspire us.

The spaciousness Harner has pointed to is a quality worth developing in our relationships as well. Creative and free space between lovers and friends, parents and children, and even in our relationship with God allows room for our unique individuality to develop. Sometimes, being apart for a time from those closest to us can strengthen our bond; as the saying goes, it "can make the heart grow fonder." Hermits like Thoreau and Merton have withdrawn from society or community to experience a "creative incubation" that ultimately makes for a more fruitful participation in the larger body. Spaciousness allows for the growth within us of creative interests and artistic expressions that we, in turn, contribute to the universe.

Incorporating more space in my relationships allows me to be more patient with my loved ones and to listen more carefully. Creating containers of spaciousness in the midst of conflict — even the brief space of taking my pulse or counting to ten — can reduce stress and ill-feelings, and increase understanding. Setting aside pockets of quiet prayer with loved ones can deepen intimacy with them as well as with God. Allowing space within the fabric of my life for the Spirit of God to work makes my efforts more creative; it also makes them more authentic.

Cultivating spaciousness in my relationships helps me to be less possessive of the ones I love. I'm less likely to contain or imprison them in my ideas about who they are and what they should be in life. The spaciousness of the stars teaches me that the attraction between us should be governed by the gravitational pull of compassion and love, not by force or coercion. To try to pull the other into the orbit of my expectations can cause a collision of wills or egos, paradoxically pulling us away from each other and from our truest selves. I need to remember that the other does not exist to fill what might be lacking in me. The other is truly a "thou," not a reflection of me.

As I return my attention to the Milky Way and its vastness, I think about how the Hubble Telescope has given us "eyes" to see into the universe's origin. Hubble also reveals great seas of galaxies that are still moving away from us in every direction. As Brian Swimme says:

> The further apart they are the faster they are moving away from each other. Galaxies twice as far apart are sailing away form each other twice as fast. Galaxies ten times as far apart sail away ten times as fast. The mathematical conclusion could not be more startling: by tracing

the trajectories of the super clusters of galaxies backward, we find an event of cataclysmic energy where a trillion galaxies are brought into a single ineffable point, the birthplace of the universe, the initial singularity of space-time, the center of the universe. There, in that place, the entire cosmos began as a pinprick, a sextillion-ton pinprick layered with the power to thunder forth into the beauty of existence.

Twelve to fifteen billion years of galactic evolution is now displayed before my eyes this night. According to Brian Swimme and Thomas Berry in their twelve-part video series *Canticle to the Cosmos,* not only am I looking at our cosmos, now the cosmos is conscious of itself in me. Swimme poetically adds, "We were once molten rock that now sings opera."

As I peer out into the heavens, I try to imagine how some beings from our neighboring Andromeda Galaxy might view us from space. I try to imagine how they might feel if they could visit this blue and white orb that is so small yet so full of diverse forms of color and life: its flowing water, refreshing rain, growing green plants, winged creatures and large land-roving animals. I imagine how they might feel if they could stand in an Amazonian rain forest and listen to the chorus of songbirds in the canopy of trees. I wonder what powers of persuasion these beings might use to convince us to halt the extinction of species and the destruction of our natural environment. Might they help us understand that each species is unique not only to earth but to the whole universe?

Perhaps they would set aside our planet as a shrine, a sacred place in space, the holy place of the universe. Indeed, our small planet nestled within two billion galaxies that stretch out into infinity is one of the great miracles of the universe. It deserves to be held in reverence and awe. Earth is like an oasis in the vast galactic black desert of the universe.

I cannot tell how much time has passed while I've been under this cosmic spell. All sense of time seemed suspended, and space opened out into infinity. As I get up and return to the lean-to, I light a candle, its soft light illuminating the log walls and hidden terrain. I get into my sleeping bag, and I savor a feeling of deep peace. The starlight is spreading through my being like a tonic, replacing the toxic effects of my too busy work-a-day world.

The spaciousness of this trek is helping to restore *susto* in my life. The wonder of this night is being diffused throughout my soul. Everyday cynicism is being replaced with positive feelings about this earth, about my life and my place in the world. Sparks of hope begin to flicker again within as I drink in vast amounts of the goodness and beauty this universe contains. Life *is* good. I am truly amazed at the reality that I even exist in this stunning universe. There is nothing in creation that demands my existence. It is simply a gift that I am here. All is gift.

Before I drift off into a sort of cocoon hibernation for the night, I want to set up some goals to embody this experience in my daily life:

◆ Try to reestablish a sense of balance between work and rest, and work and play.

◆ Make friends with the constellations and planets visible in the night sky in my area each season. Learn their names and their patterns of movement.

◆ Take time each day to stop and gaze at the sky in the early morning or the evening as a form of praise to the Creator.

◆ Invite friends to a stargazing party.

◆ Write my own version of a psalm or poem about the night sky.

◆ Try to live with a sense of spaciousness in my relationships. Create containers of spaciousness within the fabric of my life to help me recognize and cultivate more harmony and beauty in my relationships.

◆ Ponder how I can practice the prayer of quiet in order to further deepen my mystical sense of reverence and compassion for others. Incorporate pockets of prayer into my daily life to allow the Spirit of God room to work and to play.

The Web of Life

This morning I take my usual cup of coffee and move to a sunny spot in the front of the lean-to. The grasses and plants are shining wet from a brief overnight rainstorm. I sit on an old log and bask in the soft morning sunlight, slowly sipping fresh, hot black coffee from the blue, enamel-coated metal cup that's accompanied me on all my mountain treks. It's become a real companion. Sometimes I even converse with it as I sip its black contents.

While listening to the sounds and looking around at the surrounding scenery, something close by attracts my attention. It's a spider web anchored between the lean-to and some pieces of firewood stacked on the ground. I take a closer look and notice that the web begins to shimmer. Some of the lingering rain droplets start falling to the earth as a black spider emerges to claim a small flying insect stuck in its web. This truly is bad karma for the insect, but such is the daily drama in the world of nature. Each strand of the web holds dew and droplets of rain like a necklace. The light from the sun is refracted into rainbow colors by the moisture. It is indeed a precious sight.

I am awed at the intricacy and Shaker-like beauty and simplicity of what this spider has created. Each species of spider spins these geometric microfilaments with its own unique signature. Yet how thoughtlessly I overlook their artistry when I sweep webs away from porch and patio, bringing to temporary ruin the spider's whole world in a flash.

I am reminded of the Buddhist-Hindu metaphorical understanding of the net belonging to the Indian deity

Indra. At each of the vertices of this net there is a jewel. Each jewel, in turn, owes its existence to and reflects every other jewel in the net. Nothing exists alone or in isolation from other forms of life. Whatever happens to one life-form causes a shimmer throughout the entire web of life. There is a lesson here for me. Every person and thing on this earth and in the whole universe form one precious web of existence. John Muir wrote: "When we single one thing out we realize that it is connected to everything else." A Sufi saying summarizes this truth: "To pluck a flower is to trouble a star." What a realization! Looking at a simple spider's web, I have a glimpse of the entire universe. Leonardo Boff and Virgil Elizondo extend this thought into microphysics:

> All the carbon that is in our bodies, our food, the carbon dioxide in the atmosphere and limestone rocks, has already formed part of other organisms six hundred times in the process of life production. In the body of each one of us, there are about half a billion carbon atoms, which were part of the organism of persons living two thousand years ago, for example Jesus Christ. Likewise, all the nitrogen there is on the earth has already formed part of the organism of living beings and been eliminated from them approximately 800 times; the sulphur 300 times; the phosphorus 8000 times; the potassium 2000 times.

I am amazed to think that the atoms in my fingernails or in my hair may have blown in from the coast of California eight months ago — and, even more, that we earth creatures are all made up of recycled matter that is 15 billion years old! Nature produces no disposable trash; everything is recycled again and again. What dies only changes form and contributes to the life of someone or something else.

One of the Rubaiyats of Omar Kayam expresses this reality poetically:

> I sometimes think that never blows so red
> The Rose as where some buried Caesar bled;
> That every Hyacinth the Garden wears
> Dropt in its Lap from some once lovely Head.

And Hopi ceramist Al Qöawayma adds:

> We the potters are (to be) respectful of our clay.
> I know that some of this clay may even contain
> the dust of my ancestors...so...how
> Respectful I must be...and I think,
> I, too, might become part of a vessel someday!
> What a wonderful thought....
> To become useful again and to reflect the
> Creator's beauty and love.

As I now reflect, this spider's web is becoming for me like a mandala, a mystical symbol of the wholeness, totality and integrity of creation. I realize that everything in this world is held together in such a delicate balance. Interdependence and mutuality are threads of the same cord.

Larry Rasmussen, a professor of social ethics, puts it this way:

> We don't live on earth: We live as part of earth's articulation. In subtle bioregional communities we live with trees, animals, birds, and insects of nearly infinite variety; with winds, clouds, and the spirited gases of the atmosphere; with mountains, lakes, streams, oceans, beaches, forests, grasslands, and deserts; with bacteria and amoebae and viruses; with the sun, moon, and fifty billion galaxies.

Our relationship to all other communities of life-forms is mutual, and we share in and shape each other's destiny. We don't live in two separate worlds, one human the other non-human. In fact, we need to consider that the earth community might exist very well without the human species but that the human species can scarcely live without all the other living ecosystems of this earth.

Theologian Jay McDaniel explains:

> The integrity of creation refers to the value of all creatures in themselves, for one another, and for God, and their interconnectedness in a diverse whole that has unique value for God. To forget the integrity of creation is to forget that the earth itself is a splendid whole.

Native Americans like Chief Seattle and Black Elk deeply understood the principles of integrity and mutuality. They spoke about living within a delicate web of co-existent life. They not only respected other living species but even expanded their reverence to include the elements of air and earth, of rocks and mountains, of winds, sun and moon. They wisely understood that the effects of their actions extended to the seventh generation. What a sharp contrast to our adolescent-like culture with its need-centered, instant-gratification existence.

> Humankind has not
> woven the web of life.
> We are but one
> thread within it.
> Whatever we do
> to the web,
> we do to ourselves.
> All things are
> bound together.
> All things connect.
> —Chief Seattle

Creation's integrity means that the earth should be seen as a whole and that everything has a right to exist in itself. Such an awareness makes us more humble about our place in the earth community. We are only one of the marvelous strands that share life with perhaps 80 million other living species.

We humans were the last to arrive on the stage of evolutionary life on this our home planet. We appeared on the earth in the time of its fullest and most diverse display of life-forms. We literally stepped into a Garden of Eden. Modern humans have inhabited this planet for only about the last 200,000 years of earth's estimated five-billion-year lifespan. As Brian Swimme and Thomas Berry say, "In any case, we need to explain how, in a mere .00000044 percent of earth time (the last few hundred years), our species has wrought more change on the planet than had taken place in the past billion." They further suggest that "assault" rather than "communion" now names our relationship to earth. It deeply concerns me to think that we are sweeping away the other strands in our common web of existence.

Coming back to the present moment, I realize that I must take leave of these reflections if I am to reach my destination by day's end. So I part company with the spider and begin to pack up my gear for the day's hike toward Twin Brooks. I go through a mental checklist: Did I pack the flashlight, the Swiss army knife…where did I put the water bottle? This process is a precaution I've learned to practice after having left things behind on past trips.

As I start to hike, I shift the pack around on my back to find the center of gravity. The air feels cool on my skin, and sunlight is chasing down the leftover shadows of night into the underbrush of fading golden-rod and wild blue aster. My pants feel damp, but this is a small enough price to pay for today's experience.

Soon the weight of the backpack will distract me from this unpleasant feeling. The wet, muddy trail winds around a giant erratic and slopes gently upward into the woods.

Once I get into a rhythm on the path, the wheels of my mind again start to turn around my early morning encounter. My experience with the web is telling me that our ecological crisis isn't essentially about the environment at all. It's really about our values and relationships. If we view creation as object, then we can subject it to any form of treatment that suits our needs. We can abuse the rest of creation in the name of progress or maintaining a healthy short-term economy. We have fostered an *anthropocentric* life-view, placing ourselves at the center of the universe. Mystics and prophets, on the other hand, point us to a *Theocentric* view that this really is God's creation, not ours. Seeing ourselves as created in God's image calls us to cultivate and care for this earth garden as "co-creators" with God. Each living species is in some way a manifestation and expression of God's creative love. The universe story (modern science's best understanding of the universe's origins) and the story of salvation history (as recorded in Scripture) need to be woven together. When they are told as separate entities, it can lead to "apartheid thinking." This type of thinking identifies everything outside us as being foreign to us. It's not only blacks vs. whites or Jews vs. Samaritans, but human vs. non-human. And "not us" means they are less than us. As Larry Rasmussen suggests, "Such apartheid thinking leaves us imagining we are an ecologically segregated species. Such thinking violates the integrity of creation and puts it at risk."

Indeed, seeing ourselves as segregated and superior gives us permission to do whatever we please. It leaves us separate from the rest of earth's community and, ultimately, from each other and ourselves. And when it fosters the idea that God is not in the world, it leaves us separate from God. Yet a poetic, mystical vision can be an antidote to apartheid thinking.

Poets and mystics like Hildegarde of Bingen (1098-1179) help us cut through to a true vision of reality. In *The Symphony of the Harmony of Heavenly Revelations* she expressed through music and song how the Risen Cosmic Christ is at the heart of this universe. Her mandalas depict the "golden and fiery robes of the universe that hold all things together." "The man in Sapphire Blue," as she calls Christ, dwells in every person as a divine power of compassion to heal. Each creature is an image or mirror that "glistens and glitters," illuminated by the brightness of his light. The Canticle of St. Francis (1181-1226) further expresses this exuberance and deep joy in delighting at God's gift of creation: The sun is our brother; the moon is our sister. In the twentieth century priest-paleontologist Pierre Teilhard de Chardin (1881-1955) continued this tradition of appreciating our essential connection with creation and seeing Christ at the center of physical reality. Teilhard suggests that Christ is the Omega Point toward which all reality is moving. For Teilhard our world is numinous and mysterious. It displays the radiance of the divine milieu. His prayer has become mine as well: "Lord, grant that I may see You and feel Your presence in all things and animating all things." Hiking here in the mountains I understand that I am walking on sacred ground.

I feel that this Adirondack Park and all our national parks, dense forests and seashores are the playground for the mystic, poet and artist. Rachel Galvin writes about how the Adirondack region inspired Ralph Waldo Emerson and other nineteenth-century New England Transcendentalists, who believed that divinity permeated nature and all humankind. "In the wilderness we turn to reason and faith," Emerson wrote in his essay "Nature." He turned to the wilderness often, and along with some of his intellectual circle even spent a month fishing and hunting at Follensby Pond in the central Adirondacks, not far from my favorite hiking areas.

In the natural world, I find that my life force is engaged in playful — and sometimes demanding — activity, setting free a spirit of prayer and play that elsewhere is bound by routine. In backpacking, for example, arduous effort is required in climbing a mountain. But the results are expressed in celebration, as the vista of the awesome mountain peaks suddenly appears and the valleys below are filled with silence. Such awareness might release a rush of life-spirit within the soul that says, "Yes! This is it!"

My early morning encounter with the spider's web brings to mind another significant spiritual value: simplicity. Webster's Dictionary defines simplicity as "a simple state or quality; freedom from intricacy or complexity. Absence of elegance, embellishment, luxury; plainness." While this morning's web was hardly "free from intricacy" or without "elegance," these webs are pure simplicity in terms of material and design.

The shelves of bookstores are filled with volumes on the topic of "Simple Living." One of nineteenth century America's great advocates of this virtue, Henry David Thoreau, advised us to "Simplify, simplify, simplify." This became a kind of mantra for him during his residence at Walden Pond. There he sometimes sat in the doorway of his cabin and would do nothing for hours but watch a shadow being slowly chased away by the morning sunlight. Yet Thoreau's very centered existence brought great elegance to life because his deliberate lifestyle helped him find deep meaning in even the simplest activity. He chose to live unencumbered, reducing life to its bare essentials so he could live more fully.

Even closer to home, these Adirondacks have known a number of figures who withdrew from civilization to live a solitary life deep in the woods. The most celebrated of the Adirondack hermits was Noah John Rondeau. He became known as the "Mayor of Cold River" with a population of 1. Unlike other hermits, such as Ebenezer Bowen and French Louie, who were described as rather dour, Noah was friendly and outgoing. Residing in the beautiful Cold River area of the western High Peaks region, he called his cabin "Town Hall." In *Inside the Adirondack Blue Line*, Don Williams says that "It was not uncommon in an Adirondack village to see a bewhiskered, shabby, sometimes smelly old man walking into town.... He was quickly identified as the resident hermit at that settlement."

Rondeau was born in 1883 and educated himself in monk-like fashion with a supply of books stacked in his hermitage. Williams tells us that "Astronomy was his favorite subject, which he no doubt was able to put into practice on many a crisp, cool Adirondack night. He also played the violin, performing for whoever may have wandered up through the Cold River valley, or in the absence of other humans, he serenaded the deer." His spirit of Adirondack hermit simplicity is captured in this excerpt from *The Adirondack Reader*:

A visitor to his hermitage described him thus: "A pippin of a man with a face as smiley as the full moon....When he was speaking it seemed as if he was vocalizing the mystic spirit of the woods.... I could plainly see that beneath his frolicking humor there lurked a soul of rare sincerity and worth. I once heard that nature is our oldest and best teacher, and after spending those few hours with Rondeau I believe it is true.... Noah John had graduated from this unique school with a *magna cum laude* degree.

In time he became an object of great attention. The New York Department of Conservation even lifted him out by helicopter to display him at National Sportsmen shows in New York City.

The lifestyles of hermits like Rondeau and Thoreau may seem eccentric and unpractical, but they do serve as a reminder for me to live more simply, openly and reflectively. I think of the ancient Essenes and Desert Fathers and Mothers, who all took flight from a world that was growing more noisy and congested. Throughout the ages, monastic and religious communities, from the Trappists to the Shakers, have organized their communal lives around simple rules and few possessions. Like the spider web I spied this morning, the lines of these diverse communities were straightforward and direct, all intended to enable a life aligned with core values. While in their desire for simplicity some of these individuals and groups disdained beauty and held to a stark lifestyle, others wove their lives with a weblike elegance and grace.

This leads me to two quintessential questions: Around what core values is my life woven? *and* How can I simplify my life to keep the central meaning of my life in focus? In the Gospels Jesus instructs his disciples, "Take neither walking stick..." (Luke 9:3) and again "Blessed are you who have the spirit of poverty" (Matthew 5: 3). We are directed to live lives of Gospel simplicity in order to establish ourselves — and to be of service — in the reign of God. Along the same line, I believe it was Gandhi who said, "Live simply so that others may simply live."

As I look at my own life, I realize that there is too much clutter in my living space. Small piles of books, newspapers and magazines are waiting to be read. And there are so many modern advances and conveniences — from VCRs to computers — that, while they add much to life, require a great deal of time and energy to learn how to use and maintain. It's not just my possessions that complicate my life; it's also the hectic pace of my activities. Juliet Schor's study *The Overworked Americans* comments that most Americans are working longer hours than they did thirty years ago, as much as one full month more a year. We have much more than we did twenty years ago, but now we are forced to work more in order to keep it.

The instructions from the Gospels, Gandhi and others are kernels of wisdom that take a whole lifetime to understand. While I'm trying to figure them out, things keep piling up around me and I keep filling my schedule with work. It often seems like I'm too busy to think it through. At other times I feel like the rich young man from the Gospel story who "went away sad" because he could not separate himself from his many possessions (See Matthew 19: 16-22). One of my purposes in this hike is to review this fundamental question again in the hope of finding deeper insights for living a simpler lifestyle.

One thing I have discerned in this struggle to live simply is that there is a big difference between my needs and my wants. My needs are basic: some food, clothing, shelter, a job — hopefully one with meaning. My wants, however, are infinite. I can never satisfy all of them physically, emotionally or spiritually. My wants are like a consuming fire: The more I feed them, the hotter the fire burns.

The candle of this day now burned, and having covered a few miles, I decide to set my backpack down for a refreshing rest. I open a side pocket of the pack to get some gorp to indulge in. Crunchy, chewy chunks of M&M's, peanuts and raisins release their energy for my tired muscles to absorb. Sitting here alone on this trail, I find myself wishing I had a companion with whom to talk these thoughts over. This is one of those points where sharing with someone would help to deepen the reflection and focus the questions. I decide to write them down to carry them with me for future reference.

The sun is shining on the mountain peaks, and I can feel sunlight drying out my sweaty shirt where the pack pressed it against my back. The air is clear and feels warm on the skin. I am in no hurry to pick up and move on. Meanwhile, a red squirrel that was climbing up a pine tree stops, turns its head toward me and sends a loud message to the others that I have arrived in their space. I nod my head several times as if to acknowledge that fact and assure the creature that I don't intend to intrude for long. The squirrel seems to understand as he returns to his task and scampers up the tree and out of sight.

As I get ready to move on, I'm glad that the distance to the Twin Brooks area isn't too far to travel and that the trail will be on a downward slope passing Hanging Spear Falls, a favorite sight of mine. My body has moved only a few miles over ground in the last few hours, but my mind has traveled an entire galaxy in that time. The downward slope to complete the last leg of this day's hike is gentle on the knees. I pass what appears to be an "old goat" (a pit where now-rusted tin cans, discolored bottles and other refuse were dumped by hikers years ago). Arriving at level ground, I find a clearing to set up my tent for the night and begin to prepare supper. I think I hear the faint flow of running water close by. I will explore later. I unpack my portable "kitchen." An envelope of chicken and rice looks like a good choice for supper.

After a meal cooked and eaten very unceremoniously,

I dig out my leather tramp journal to review and record the insights of the day. I am grateful to the spider whose simple web made me more aware of the entire universe. Some points distilled for reflection are:

♦ What does Gospel simplicity mean for me as a way of life?

♦ What are some things I can do to simplify my life? How can I unclutter my living space and lifestyle?

♦ What unthinking patterns in my day-to-day routine can I reevaluate to break the cycle of overactivity?

♦ How can I live simply so that others might simply live?

♦ How can I deepen my awareness of the impact my choices as a consumer have on the web of life?

♦ How can I adjust my prayer life and my patterns of activity so I might more deeply respect and appreciate my connection within the web of life?

Majestic Mountains and Shooting Stars

It's not uncommon for me to awaken before dawn when I am sleeping outdoors. It seems that my body takes on the cicada-like rhythm of the birds that begin their morning chant in that still period prior to the light of dawn. Since it's not raining, I get up to view the pre-dawn sky aglow with stars and planets.

This morning the Quarter Moon, with her royal attendants, Venus and Jupiter, is lying low on the horizon, watching the slow circle dance of the constellations in her heavenly courtyard. Earth's shadow still veils her secret beauty from sight. What a grand and spectacular way to begin the day! It speaks of Daniel Berrigan's version of Psalm 8:

> The heavens bespeak the glory of God.
> The firmament ablaze, a text of God's works.
> Dawn whispers to sunset.
> Dark to dark the word passes: glory glory.

Meanwhile, jet black silhouettes of the Colden and Avalanche Mountains stand silently against the background of the deep, dark sky. These silent and strong sentinels of time remain solidly firm through the change of seasons and the passage of the centuries. The Adirondacks have a long history dating back some 1.2 billion years when the bedrock that composed the Adirondacks was formed. This rock, known as anthrosite, is exceptionally strong and is very rare on earth (though it is commonplace on the moon). Its strength enabled the mountains to survive the advancing and receding glaciers.

Immovable and majestic, mountains withstand whatever comes. What powerful symbols of faith: Mountains convey strength and trust in weathering the storms of life. It's no wonder so many ancient religions believed that their gods dwelt on the mountaintops. Not only were their peaks at the point of touching the heavens, they were perceived to be unshakable and imperishable.

Many Scripture passages use mountains to describe religious experiences. For example, Moses, the fiery prophet Elijah and Jesus each withdrew into the mountains to pray. Peter, James and John had a profound experience of the divine on the Mount of Transfiguration. Muhammad often retired to a cave on the summit of Mount Hira, where he fasted, prayed and gave alms to the poor. Similarly, Black Elk had religious visions on a mountaintop.

Thinking about these famous figures meeting God on the mountaintop makes me realize that there are two things one should not undertake lightly: namely, climbing a mountain and praying "Thy will be done." Earnestly pronouncing this phrase from the Our Father is like writing a blank check that can cost us all that we are. At the very least it can cause lasting changes in one's life. Moses shrunk before the face of Yahweh, and Jesus' disciples of were terrified at the Transfiguration. Muhammad woke on his mountain to find himself overpowered by a devastating presence, which squeezed him tightly until he heard the first words of the new Muslim Scriptures pouring from his lips. One should tread lightly on such places. Mountaintop theophanies can have all the intensity of facing a grizzly or entering a blast furnace.

Like those who have encountered God in the

mountains, the mountains themselves are often shaken. In the daylight one can notice the face of many mountains scarred from raging storms that assaulted them in the past. Giant Mountain (elevation 4,627feet) is one that comes to mind. In the 1960s a *perfect storm* converged on Giant. For 90 minutes, three thunderstorms locked in on its summit, bringing torrential rains that washed trees, soil, rocks and vegetation down the west face of the mountain into the ravine below. The flow of debris continued until it filled the ravine and then climbed up its walls before covering the highway. The road was closed for three days while work crews cleared it. Yet, all that destruction damaged only the face of the mountain; the deep interior remained peacefully still and untouched. Isn't that a wonderful image of what a strong faith can do for us? With faith we can weather life's storms. Though our problems and failures lash at us, with deep faith we can endure and stand strong through it all. In the interior of our soul we can find the strength to hold on until the storm passes and not be swept away.

In stark contrast to the enduring stability of the mountains is another natural reality displayed in the early morning. Above the peaks of the Colden and Avalanche Mountains I catch sight of, at different intervals, *shooting stars* passing in the still black sky. These dramatic displays of flaring light that suddenly appear and quickly fade into cosmic extinction give rise to a poignant thought: We are like shooting stars that make our bright appearance in the cosmos and then just as suddenly vanish from sight. In the words of Walt Witman:

> As I flit through you hastily,
>   soon to fall and be gone,
>   what is this chant?
> What am I myself but one of your meteors?

A question I recently read flashes into my awareness: If I had an hour to live and could make one phone call, whom would I call and what would I say? This is a very probing question. It may seem dramatic, but it serves to focus our attention on other quintessential questions. Who really matters to me? Who in my journey of life has made a significant, lasting impression and has found a way into the inner chambers of my heart? To whom would I express my affection, gratitude and love? Finally, and pointedly, how would I like to spend the last few hours of my life on earth?

I once attended a workshop on the rite of Christian funeral liturgy and burial. The speaker asked us what was the most important thing inscribed on a tombstone? You can guess the range of answers. Some said it was the epitaph, which is a summary of a person's life; others said it was the name. I was surprised when the presenter said that, for him, the most important thing was the *hyphen*. It was the brief span of time between the dates of birth and death. As Psalm 90 says:

> Make us know the shortness of our life
> that we may gain wisdom of heart.

Recently, I was talking with a friend whom I had not seen for a many months. We started checking names of mutual acquaintances so we could update each other. When we review our lists together, we almost always begin by mentioning someone who has died. It seems natural to do this before sharing the news of a new birth, a birthday or a new job one of our friends may be celebrating.

Then my friend told me about a religious sister in her community who was having headaches and went to see a doctor. After tests, she was told that she had an inter-cranial aneurysm and that no operation was possible. Adding to this shocking news was the fact that a bleed could occur any time — within a week or even an hour. The doctor encouraged her to consider checking into a hospital. The sister thought about the suggestion but decided to go home and go about her normal activities for as long as she had time left. She would continue to live the day with its simple pleasures and joys, with its tedious routine, with its struggles and surprises. She lived four more days before the aneurysm ended her earthly life just as she was about to take a shower. She must have prepared herself for that moment long before it occurred. There was no panic, no frantic pace to suddenly accomplish something before she died. She faced the situation with a faith the size of a mountain, remaining calm and courageous in the storm.

I wonder how I would react if I got that same news today. This kind of quintessential question can quickly bring things into focus.

Usually, we avoid thinking of our own mortality. We live in a culture that denies death and hides it from view. We focus our attention on the vitality and energy of youth. We seldom use the word *death* in our conversations, ordinarily substituting euphemisms like *passed away* or *went to sleep*. Yet, isn't it true that knowing we are going to die makes the time we have with each other so much more precious?

On this particular hike, autumn is in full display around me. I'm struck by how nature, which is ablaze with vivid colors and seems most spectacular during this season, is in the act of dying during the fall. It's as if all the vitality of nature moves onto center stage to make a lasting impression on us before she dies. Those who have time to prepare for their own death peacefully have the opportunity to review the colors of their life among us, assuring them before they die that they will not be forgotten. When our loved ones die consciously and gracefully — mirroring the beauty of autumn — it enables us to carry the lasting memories of their lives with us.

Moreover, thinking deeply about our mortality can motivate us toward a new way of living each day. I can put my priorities into alignment and bring them into full view. My deep-down soul values get moved to the top of the *to do* list. I don't take today for granted, and I appreciate more the presence of the people around me.

In the movie *Dead Poets Society*, photographs of past alumni are hanging on the darkened walls of the school. The question is asked: If they could come back from the dead, what would they tell us? The answer is *Carpe diem*! Seize the day! This expression from the *Odes of Horace*, the classic Roman writer, tells us to live this moment fully. Be present to it all with your full attention. Tether your mind to the now. Suck the marrow out of the bone of life today. How often we live in the past or the future instead of totally engaging our life in this moment.

Living the present moment, fully aware of our mortality, can be the key to inner joy and gratitude for the gift of life I have today. It invites me to wear my life loosely as a garment, not to take myself too seriously and to take no one and nothing for granted. It's an invitation to enjoy the people and simple events that make up this day.

We've all have heard about someone who was going to begin living his or her life after retiring, or when the kids had grown up or after having collected enough money. How many times have we compromised doing the truly important things in order to accomplish lesser goals? Too often we delay developing true intimacy in our marriages or put off spending time in prayer to cultivate our relationship with God. We can postpone spending time with friends, taking a vacation with family or a fishing trip with the kids because we're too busy now and think we'll always have time for those "extras" in the future. How often have we put off spending time with a favorite hobby or learning a new one, or put off taking long walks or just sitting quietly listening to music, all because of a sense of urgency about the next task on our list. Yet poets, mystics and prophets remind us that it's important to count more sunsets, take more risks and laugh more. They challenge us to address real problems rather than merely thinking about imaginary ones or getting stuck in petty ones.

We all know the truism that you'll never hear a dying person say he or she should have spent more time at the office. Yet we really need to listen to the wisdom in this. We need to make up our own set of priorities and then live by them. As I think about the shooting star that quickly comes into view and fades in the night sky, I wonder how my family and friends will remember me? What will the world remember of me? What beautiful qualities will I leave behind for others to recall about me?

I once gave a workshop at which I asked the participants to do this exercise: Draw a straight line on a sheet of paper representing the length of years you think you will live. At the beginning of the line put the number "1"; at the end of the line put the number that represents the last year of your life (I put 85). Now intersect this line at the point where you are now living and figure what percentage of your life is left to live. Then under this graph list those things that are important for you to do before you die. Remembering how little time you have left to do those things, start making plans to accomplish them today.

The trail on today's trek has been wet and muddy. It now veers away from a small brook and comes to what looks like an old lumber clearing. It proceeds up an easy grade, passing between two large erratics. As I climb a bit, another mountain range, perhaps part of the MacIntyre Range, comes into view in the distance. From this spacious mountaintop perspective I can embrace both my fleeting mortality and the promise of eternal life inherent in Jesus' transfiguration and resurrection. The trail grade begins to get steeper as it makes its way up among rocks and boulders, passing around a large blowdown. Down below, I spot a grassy meadow and brook. It looks like a good enough place to camp out for the night.

Before setting out the tent and rolling out the sleeping bag, I pause to sit and drink some water, which now in low supply. As I set out to find a water source close by to filter and refill my water bottles before dark, I reflect on how this eighth mile of my hike has awakened me to some powerful insights that I feel will be life changing. Upon returning and setting up camp, I begin to think about my evening meal. Among my food trove I find an envelope of chili with rice and beans. With some boiling water this dry clay-like powder should be transformed into a delightful meal.

After dinner, everything now squared away for the evening, I record some points for reflection:

♦ Draw a new "lifeline" and see where I am on that line.

♦ Make of list of things that are important for me to accomplish before I die.

♦ Identify my fears about death and dying and work toward integrating my fears within my life view and purpose.

♦ List five things I've done in my life that I consider valuable and that have made a difference to others.

♦ How can I keep my personal *end time* in focus so

as to use this *now time* to its greatest advantage?

♦ How do I begin to cultivate a strong, mountain-like faith so that I won't be deterred by life's storms?

♦ Can I find deeper inner calm and greater life resources by developing my practice of prayer and meditation?

Side Trip to Skylight Mountain

When I awoke this morning, I knew that I was in the backcountry, more by the feeling on my skin than by any other outward sign. After four or five days of hiking, the entire surface of a tramper's skin has that crawling sensation, like microscopic creatures are boring in through every pour. This *seasoning* of the skin means that one has crossed the threshold of civilized societal standards of cleanliness into the unkempt company of the former "peakbaggers" of this wilderness area. I think of the legendary Adirondack guide Old Mountain Phelps (circa 1850), a man who was known as a "hater of soap." Seneca Ray Stoddard describes him in these terms:

> A little man, about five feet six in height, muffled up in an immense crop of long hair and a beard that seemed to boil up out of his collar band. Grizzly as the granite ledges he climbs, shaggy as the rough-barked cedar, but with a pleasant twinkle in his eye and an elasticity to his step equaled by few younger men. He likes to talk and delivers his sage conclusions and whimsical oddities in a cheery, chirrupy, squeaky sort of tone — away up on the mountain as it were — an octave above the ordinary voice, somewhat suggestive of the warbling of an ancient chickadee.

In *The Wilderness* Charles Dudley Warner added, "His clothes seemed to have been put on him once and for all, like the bark of a tree, a long time ago."

After Warner's article about him appeared in *The Atlantic* that same year, he became famous and started posturing to the public. Summing up a not-uncommon belief that his skills as a guide were greatly overstated, Mary MacKenzie of the North Elba Historical Historical Association referred to him as "that wily scamp."

Verplanck Colvin, who measured the elevations of many high peaks, is another backcountry character. Philip Terrie, a student of Adirondack history described Colvin as a "crank" and "as loony as they come." A lifelong teetotaler, he was known for his offbeat behavior. Terrie tells the story of one occasion: "When lobbying for appointment to the Adirondack survey job, Colvin invited some fifty influential politicians to a grand reception, at which he served no food and no drink, but only ice water. Though the guests were outraged and left early, Colvin thought the party a grand success."

Living in the backcountry does have a cost, both socially and on the level of personality. Yet, despite all their quirks and coarse ways, Colvin, Mountain Phelps and two other peakbaggers *were* the first of European descent to climb Skylight Mountain in 1873. And, perhaps more importantly, in varying degrees they became one with the mountains and absorbed the wonder and beauty of the backcountry.

As I prepare to hike through the backcountry this morning, I feel I would have been good company for these eccentrics and "haters of soap." While musing on these mountain legends, I rub the tramper's skin on my left forearm and then fire up my faithful small Siva stove to make breakfast. With some fine-tuning the flame burns light blue, perfect for brewing some black coffee and instant oatmeal with raisins. A granola power-bar will serve as a delicious side dish. What a wonderful way to start the day: sitting by the Opalescent

River holding a mug of hot coffee with both hands and watching the filtered sunlight slide down the outer log wall of the lean-to and then spread across the wet forest floor. Morning arrives silently and stealthily as a cat.

The sound of this gentle river is soothing and brings relief to my crawling skin problem. The Opalescent begins as a trickling stream on the north side of Tahawus and spills into the Flowed Lands, continuing on until its confluence with the Hudson River about 8 miles from this spot. Even the name *opalescent* — meaning milky and iridescent like an opal — seems fitting for the indirectness of this morning. The river's water is not actually milky, but perhaps it was named when the snow pack was melting, which can give the waters a turbid appearance. Unlike the mountain ranges of the West, the Adirondacks aren't subject to the movement of thick glaciers that grind the surface rock into a fine powder. The glacier flour of the Rockies is carried off into the rivers and streams, giving the water an opalescent cast.

In keeping with the spirit of the Opalescent, I've been thinking about taking an unplanned side trip to the top of Skylight (4,926 feet) for a day of diversion. Rather than my usual frontal assault on my quintessential questions, it feels like a time for a more indirect approach to my quest. I'd like to make this a day of the *senses*, a day of living on the *surface of the skin* instead of in the deep canyons of my mind. I'm reminded of some lines in "The Spiritual Power of Matter" from Teilhard de Chardin's *Hymn of the Universe*:

> You thought you could do without it (matter) because the power of thought has been kindled in you? You hoped the more thoroughly you rejected the tangible, the closer you would be to spirit?... Never, if you work to live and grow will you be able to say to matter, "I have seen enough of you; I have surveyed your mysteries

and have taken from them enough food for my thought to last me forever."

While all the mental composting along this trek has been fruitful, today I want to focus on being attentive to all the sensations of earth, sky, wind and sounds in this mountain cathedral. Like the Vietnamese Buddhist Thich Nhat Hanh, who teaches that the present moment contains the seeds of all things, I want to practice an earthy *mindfulness* on this day's hike.

It's been my experience that when consciously living on the surface of the skin, a good spirit comes to sweep the soul free from accumulated debris, from cobwebs of past problems, from the dust of old, persistent worries. When I return from such times, I find the interior of the soul refreshingly clean and well ventilated. In the words of John Muir:

> Climb the mountains and get their good tidings. Nature's peace will flow into you as sunshine flows into trees. The winds will blow their own freshness into you, and the storms their energy, while cares will drop off like autumn leaves.
>
> Keep close to Nature's heart...and break clear away, once in awhile, and climb a mountain or spend a week in the woods. Wash your spirit clean.

It's paradoxical that becoming a peakbagger — a "hater of soap" who gets out into nature's wilderness areas — can "wash the soul clean." Moreover, simply breaking with our routines and taking a long walk in the woods can restore vitality to the soul. A day of hiking in the wilderness practicing the spiritual art of mindfulness can help free us from the dungeon of workaholism and the self-imposed demands of job or family. It can bring us up for some fresh air on the surface of our skin. Even more, the perspective of the mountains can bring balance to our lives. This practice of washing the soul clean may be one of the most challenging spiritual disciplines for our time.

Checking my "topo" map, I see that the summit to Skylight is not a long or difficult trek, just a short half mile off the main trail to the top. It won't tax my body and cause a bone marrow meltdown. Besides, it's more off the beaten path than the other option, Mt. Marcy, which is also 5,344 feet in elevation.

I lace on my damp boots and stuff a small backpack with a meager supply of dried fruit, cheese and gorp (good old raisins and peanuts). I discover that the noise I'd heard periodically through the night was the activity of some pine martens who ate their way through my "protected" food cache suspended by rope from a tree limb. Yet I don't mind sharing some of my food with them since they're now listed as an endangered species.

Filtering some drinking water from the river, I leave base camp to walk in the footsteps of Old Mountain Phelps, Verplanck Colvin and company to become a peakbagger for the day. I recall a line from *Zen and the Art of Motorcycle Maintenance* about the journey *being* the destination. So I remind myself: Be aware of what is happening all along the way. There's so much going on all around you all the time. Be attentive!

In a short time I arrive at the *four corners*, the junction of the Elk Lake and Calamity Brook trails to Tahawus. From here it's only a quarter mile hike to the open well-rounded dome at the summit of Skylight. There my eyes will feast on an impressive panorama of thirty other high peaks. But for now I bring my attention back to what's right under my feet: this wet, well-eroded metamorphic and igneous rocky terrain. The climbing grade is easy and passes through an open alpine meadow and through some thick conifers.

As the trail emerges from under the fir trees, I can

feel the sunlight on my face. Small pyramid-like piles of stones called *cairns* now mark the pathway to the summit. These silent sages mark the trail for those who hike above the tree line. There is a common belief that if one fails to carry a small stone to the top, it will rain. I mentally barter with the gods, promising to carry two the next time. As I climb, I stop frequently to look around, taking in deep breaths and drinking in the expansive vistas. Though it's still quite early in the day, I can see some climbing human figures near the summits of Tahawus and Haystack. After the timberline is reached, the rest of the climb to the bare summit is easy. Although it's not physically demanding, the ascent is energizing. My pulse is beating strongly, and blood is coursing through my veins as my lungs are filled with crisp mountain air. A feeling of good health and vitality pervades my body.

Here on the summit it is unseasonably warm, bright and sunny for autumn. Since no one else is around, I decide to take off some of my wet articles of clothing to let them dry in the sunlight and wind. The breeze might also carry away some of the tiny stowaway creatures in between the fibers of my sweat-soaked shirt and faded jeans. Then, I sit down on top of this summit in my shorts and socks, in complete awe of all that lies exposed below me. I can think of no other place I would rather be. My senses are saturated, and the tormented terrain of my dermal cells is now soothed and rejuvenated.

I recall the first time I learned to *pray* from the surface of my skin. I credit mosquitoes for teaching me this form of prayer. My friends Tom, Tim and I drove to a remote lake in the Adirondack Mountains for a day of canoeing. Due to high humidity and heat we found that we were easy game for the swarming squadrons of female anopheles. They mercilessly attacked our exposed bodies as we carried the canoe overhead through dense forest. I can't imagine why

Dante left this form of earthly torment out of his inferno.

We lost no time launching into the cool waters of the calm lake that day, our faces into the warming sun and gentle breeze. We were alone in this vast expanse of blue sky, green forest and cool water. It felt uniquely refreshing and very primitive. A mile from the launch site we stopped at a rocky point for a swim and lunch. I was the first to plunge into the silken waters of the mountain lake. The water immediately became a healing balm, soothing the mosquito bites and tired muscles. It was then that I first experienced the surface of my skin as a semi-permeable membrane to the soul. Swimming in that lake was like being in the womb of the universe. My soul was feasting on all the sensations of life in the wilderness. I was being transformed from a complaining creature into a praying one. I listened to myself almost automatically praying the Canticle of Daniel: "You trees and cedars, bless the Lord…mountains and hills praise the Lord, lakes and rivers praise and exalt God forever."

What a wondrous summer day we spent together. There wasn't as much talking as there was splashing and kicking and laughing and shouting out: Wow! Wonderful! Casual observers nearby surely would have suspected that some berserkers had taken possession of us. Yet as St. Irenaeus wrote, "The glory of God is a person fully alive." We were certainly giving God glory in a most primal way at that moment, as much as any cloistered monk in adoration anywhere on the earth. The adjacent lines of Teilhard's *Hymn of the Universe* cited above sum up my exuberance on that day:

> Son of earth, steep yourself in the sea of matter,
> bathe in its fiery waters, for it is the source of
> your life and your youthfulness.

There's something blessed about the grime of a tramper's skin. It reflects entering into our earthly domain adequately to have truly accepted the reality of natural, material existence — feeling at home in our body and the world. That acceptance, in turn, paradoxically enables the surface of our skin to become a semi-permeable spiritual membrane, so that there is no barrier to seeing all of creation as part of the Body of Christ. Again, Teilhard, from the "Mass of the World":

> *Ut nobis Corpus et Sanguis fiat*...(that it may become for us the Body and Blood of Christ). If I firmly believe that everything around me is the body and blood of the Word, then for me is brought about that marvelous diaphany which causes the luminous warmth of a single life to shine forth from every event, every element.... How I long, Lord Christ, for this to be! May my acceptance be ever more complete...my being ever more open and transparent to your influence.

A scurrying chipmunk brings my attention back to this summit place. All the natural healing elements of air and sunlight are passing through the surface of my skin into the inner chambers of my soul. The increasing energy finds expression in high praise to God.

I'm living this present moment fully. My senses and my soul are filled with this mountain, this air, this sunlight. The waning warmth of autumn envelops me and penetrates my skin. Lying on a giant granite slab, I feel the sun's radiant heat stored in these stones passing deeply into me. A first class sauna! I marvel at how praying from the surface of my skin involves my whole being. Life seems so sweet. I once again offer my prayers of praise to a playful Creator.

The hours have gently passed; they've been saturated with a sense of the timeless. Somewhat reluctantly I recognize that it's time to return to base camp. I want to go back slowly, without rush. I want to savor this moment and carry off this summit my experience of a day lived fully. Later I will reflect more about its spiritual significance.

When I reach my base camp lean-to, I find some scurrying little creatures waiting for me like a faithful canine friend might greet its master at the door. It won't be dark for a while yet, so I decide to just relax and slowly prepare something for supper. Looking through my pack, I pull out an envelope of spaghetti with sauce. Along with this treat, I'll make some soup to "warm up the innards," as Old Mountain Phelps would say. Usually I think these food envelopes should state that the flavors are sealed out, not in. Yet at the moment I'm more hungry than I am a backpacker food critic, so I'll feast sumptuously on this lightweight load of carbohydrates. Whenever I come into the backcountry, I also bring along a few of those 4 oz. bottles of cheap red wine that airlines pass on to flyers. Tonight I'll sip some fruit of the vine with dinner and save the rest for a custom that I refer to as "*wine-ing* down the day."

The spaghetti and sauce proved to be an unexpectedly fine meal. Dinner was delightful, but darkness is closing in. So I stow away the food cache, knowing that the pine martens will visit again during the night. This time I devise a suspension system instead of hanging the cache of groceries on a line straight down from the limb. I use the last bit of daylight to arrange the sleeping bag, air mattress, flashlight, candle and red wine for the night. Then I find my pen and leather tramp journal to record some notes.

Wine-ing down the day is a ritual I've practiced sporadically over the years. It's an adaptation of one of the spiritual exercises of St. Ignatius of Loyola (1491). I take time for a conscious spiritual review of the day to see just where God has been speaking and acting in the people and events that have unfolded during my waking hours. It's kind of like God is sitting on the porch in a rocking chair listening and talking with me about these events in an informal way.

There have been many modern interpretations of Ignatius' exercise now commonly called the *consciousness examine*. In my ritual adaptation of this spiritual exercise for use by leather tramps, I light a candle, pour a glass of wine (hot tea also works) and sit in a comfortable chair. I then become aware of God's presence here "on the porch" and review my day, starting with the first waking moments. It is an open conversation with God about the challenges, failures and blessings that have been part of the fabric of my life during the past 16 or 18 hours. The exercise always ends with a prayer of gratitude.

This discipline has been a most important practice in my spiritual life. So many treasures can be discovered buried in the field of everyday life. Sometimes a pearl of great price can be found, some really valuable experience that was overlooked at the moment. I recall times of spiritual healings or when I've felt added strength to undertake new challenges in ministry or when I've experienced a deeper sense of compassion for others. When consciously attended to, each of these times nurtures a sense of gratefulness. The kind of mindfulness that wine-ing down the day affords me naturally leads to a full response of the heart for what is *gratis*, freely given. Such a response comes almost spontaneously to the awareness of such pure grace.

Some of the light from the candle in my lean-to swirls around inside my glass of wine, illuminating its redness at the center of this night. William Blake wrote about seeing "a world in a grain of sand"; I now see many miracles for which to be grateful reflected in this cup of red wine. My side trip to Skylight has allowed me to spend this day in a leisurely and fully conscious way, surfacing important insights. I make a short list of things I might want to review for further practice:

- Again, get out for more long, leisurely walks in the woods or hikes in the mountains.

- If it's true that soap separates us from reality, I'd like to create more opportunities to become one with the elements and pray from the surface of my skin.

- Practice more earthy mindfulness and recognize all matter as part of the Body of Christ.

- Practice that same kind of awareness in the "nitty-gritty" circumstances of daily life.

- Allow the Word of God and the Eucharist to saturate the permeable membranes of my soul more consciously and more often.

- Set aside time most every evening to "wine down" and review the day.

- Listen to Brother David Steindl-Rast's tape on Gratitude of the Heart — a particularly beautiful reflection on gratefulness.

- Cultivate moments of gratefulness throughout each day and show real appreciation to others for things great and small.

- Remember that life is too short to drink cheap wine.

It seems fitting to end this day with a favorite prayer by G.K. Chesterton:

Gratitude

Here lies another day
during which I have had eyes,
ears, hands and the great
world around me, and
tomorrow begins another.
Why am I allowed two?

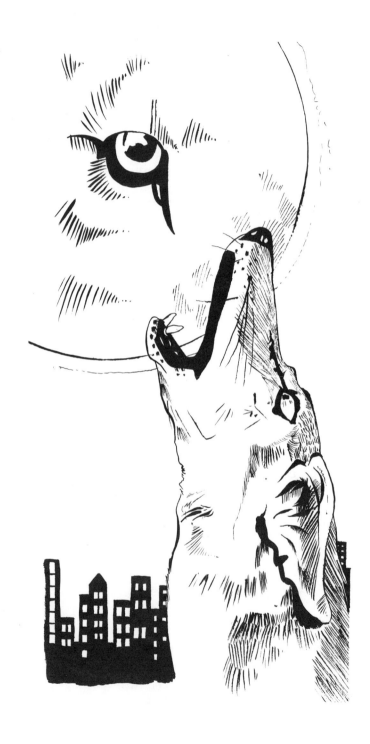

Mile Ten

The Backcountry and the Call of the Wild

Today I'd like to enjoy just "hanging out" for an extra day here in the backcountry. The Flowed Lands, Mt. Colden, Calamity Mountain, the Opalescent River, Avalanche Pass — all have their own backcountry lure. Like yesterday, however, I don't feel up to bagging any high peaks (those over 4,000 feet in altitude). I want to settle into this space and savor the feeling of being surrounded by beauty. I want to hike as a "flatlander" today and do some tramping in the level areas of the backcountry instead of on the mountaintops. So, after a light breakfast and a savored cup of coffee, I gather a few provisions in my daypack and take off on a gentle trail.

Hiking and camping in the Adirondack backcountry started to become popular in the 1930s and 1940s. Many people took to the woods for a weekend of quiet nights and days under sun and stars. Previously, the only white people to venture into the interior of what was considered an unsuitable wilderness were trappers making a living selling pelts of beaver and otter. Some of the earliest backcountry hikers were drawn to the Adirondacks after a Congregational minister from Boston, William H.H. Murray, wrote his book *Adventure in the Wilderness* in 1869. In it, he described romantic and daring stories about hunting, fishing and canoeing on the remote rivers and lakes. This attracted to the mountains crowds of people who were totally unequipped and physically unfit to face the weather, insects, impenetrable terrain and lack of places to stay. This band of disciples became know as "Murray's Fools."

Writers and painters continued to create romantic notions about the Adirondacks as a place where city dwellers seeking physical conditioning and spiritual health could come for what was not available to them in their soft civilized lives. Hiking clubs proliferated, and the *call of the wild* was responded to by urban dwellers from as far away as Long Island Sound, New Jersey and Connecticut. Wilderness Societies and Mountain Clubs opened the floodgates to large numbers of weekend trampers. Laura and Guy Waterman note that:

> The Adirondacks enjoyed a burst of popularity when the third and last of the great Northeastern mountain clubs appeared, the Adirondack Mountain Club. In his 1921 keynote address, State Forester Howard proposed three fundamental objectives:
> 1. Stimulate interest in the out-of-doors and encourage hiking and camping.
> 2. By the development of trails and campsites, open up a wider field and increase the pleasure of those who have heard the call of the wild.
> 3. Improve the camping manners of the public.

The boom would accelerate some years later as the increased availability of cars and newly constructed highways got people to within a few miles of their wilderness destinations. Soon more trails were developing into the backcountry and over mountaintops, helping to eliminate the "herd paths" made by individuals tramping their own trails into the mountains. Shelter construction began with the building of lodges and the legendary Adirondack open-front lean-to. The opening of these shelters gave hikers access to the high peak region and tied together the separated trail systems.

I am amused and amazed by accounts of early trampers. Typically, they slept on beds of balsam boughs. An army blanket served as both sleeping bag and backpack; belongings were rolled up in the blanket and carried over one's shoulders. Hikers wore sneakers rather than hiking boots, and food was cooked by campfire, usually on a black iron skillet. The smoke was heavy, and open fires blackened everything used for cooking. Hiking gear was neither fancy nor light.

While the style of these trampers seems primitive, whenever I am preparing for a backcountry trip I think of the Huaorani, a tribe of Amazonian Indians who truly get down to basics. Adult males can travel for a week or two through the rain forest wearing just what they have on; they find all they need to survive along the way. It has taken me years of hiking experience to learn that even one extra ounce can make my backpack into an atlas-load when I'm doing a vertical ascent. My consumer conditioning tempts me to go into the mountains as a tourist with all my creature comforts instead of as pilgrim with only what I need.

As I hike on today's backcountry trail, I've enjoyed the easy grade that's passed over a few gentle knolls before leveling out again. It seems that now, however, the terrain is beginning to shift. I spot a large bolder that has split and formed a crevice. Passing a *vlei*, a wet grassy area, I notice a good deal of deterioration. After crossing an outlet, I eventually reach the northwest shoreline of Lake Colden. I want to catch the impressive view of the bare rockslide of Colden with the Trap Dike. The deep clef of the Trap Dike caused by erosion is explored by adventuresome hikers striving to get to the top of the mountain.

Not long into this part of the hike, some early

childhood memories begin to surface. I recall days of carefree play after school, running with other neighborhood kids through the fields of high grasses and woods on narrow dirt trails, imagining that wild animals were about to leap upon us. I remember the laughter and echoes of fright resounding in the caves that we discovered high on the banks of the Mohawk River. Our sandlot baseball field became a mud-lot after a rainfall, and our sneakers got clogged an inch thick with the stuff. I remember coming home after a full day of playing outdoors, grass-stained and caked with dirt from our great outdoor adventures. We looked like we were just uncovered from an archeological dig. It was a great feeling to be immersed in the natural world around us.

Those fields and woods were replaced by a condo development. The caves have been backfilled for a parking lot. Our sandlot diamond is now a fenced-in little league field with a well-manicured lawn. There are so few spontaneous sports activities for kids today, fewer fields where they can run free in the sunlight and wind like the wild mustangs of the Plains. I wonder what is being gained by the highly structured and competitive social life of children today. Might we not be domesticating their imaginative powers and bridling their spontaneous expressions of childhood life? In a world where games are played on a computer screen or in video parlors, "child's play" is fast becoming *virtual* adventure rather than *real* adventure.

Further into today's trek, the trail descends into Avalanche Pass. Though my intention this day was again to stay on the surface of the backcountry, I feel myself being inexorably drawn deeper into the wilderness. This trail follows the MacIntyre Range, the peaks of which rise loftily against the sky. Many consider the MacIntyres to be the most awesome group of mountains in the

Adirondacks, which makes them the subject of many photographers. I set out for one of my favorite spots, Avalanche Lake, which lies between precipitous Mt. Colden and Avalanche Mountain. It is a tricky trail to hike; one has to use hands and feet to climb the ledges, plank walks, ladders and log bridges. These narrow plank walks over water are known as "Hitch-up Matildas." As the story goes, legendary guide Bill Nye once carried a lady customer on his back across this spot, and as the water rose higher, he warned her to protect her skirt. His phrase, "Hitch-up Matilda," has been used to describe these sections of trail ever since.

I'm attracted to a faint echo of "water music" flowing somewhere off the trail ahead. It's a refreshing sound for a tired body to listen to. It lures me into a harsher terrain than I wanted to deal with today, given my low energy. But, as Outward Bound says, "If you can't get out of it, get into it." And now I *am* into it. I sense the Spirit at work in my intuitions, luring me into the wilderness long before my mind had an inkling as to why I was coming to this spot. Could it be that my soul has been looking for a special place to meet with me? A passage from the Book of Hosea comes to mind: "That is why I am going to lure her and lead her out into the wilderness and speak to her heart" (Hosea 2: 16-17). Yahweh lured Israel into the desert, the spiritual wilderness, to speak radically to her heart. There is something elemental about wilderness places like the one I'm immersed in right now. There are fewer distractions; one focuses on the root realities of life, even on the very issue of survival.

The call of the wild reminds me of a time a few years ago when someone gave me a free trip to Jackson Hole, Wyoming. I wanted to explore the Grand Tetons and do some cross-country skiing in the parks there. One late afternoon after a full day of skiing, I decided to take some pictures of the setting sun from one of the peaks on Teton Pass. I drove to the site and parked my car. No one else was around. I began to ski westward up a gentle grade on the spine of the mountain in the fresh powder. Upon arriving at the first peak, an entire vista of snow-covered summits appeared with deep, shadow-filled valleys in between. The sun was beginning to take on the appearance of a giant orange as it descended above the high, pointed peaks. In that expansive space It felt like I was the only human being on this earth. The isolation and exhilaration was enchanting as I beheld the frozen world before me. Wanting the best possible vantage point to snap the photos, I set out toward the next peak for a better shot at the setting sun. It wasn't a difficult climb, and the glide was good, given the frigid temperatures and dry powder conditions. When I arrived, I found still another peak a short distance away. But because this spot was so breathtaking, I resisted the urge to ski to the next ridge.

I stood in awe with my back to the wind as the setting sun spread its deep reddish-orange glow over the snow-capped peaks. Even though I didn't want to disconnect from the experience before me, I took some pictures as the sun passed out of sight below the mountains. All that remained was a slight ember glow that illuminated the horizon. It would be dark soon, and I knew it was time to get going. I put my camera away and turned around to find a half-moon rising in the eastern sky. I suddenly realized that I had lost all tracers of my return path. Snowdrifts had covered my ski tracks. It was getting darker and colder, and looking at the diverging paths before me, I realized that I was lost! It wasn't easy to control my feelings of panic. Look! Think! Stay calm! Stay calm! These became my survival mantras. I had no water, flashlight, food, matches or map. All I had on my back was my camera.

I picked a path that looked like it might be the one I had climbed to the get to the spine of the mountain. As I telemarked halfway down the slope in knee-deep powder, I realized it was the wrong choice. Again, the adrenaline rushed through my body. My mind was racing at the speed of light in all directions. What could I do? Since I had been skiing all day, I began to wonder if I would have enough energy to climb back to the top in this deep snow. Without liquids and nourishment would my electrolytes remain stable, or would I just collapse in the snow? Should I build a snow cave as shelter for the night? Could I survive the below-freezing temperatures?

I slowly began my way back up the slope at a gradual angle to mitigate the steepness. Less than twenty yards into the climb I discovered the ski tracks of someone who must have skied through earlier in the day. I was filled with hope, believing that it would lead me out. I felt a new energy surge as I climbed back up. By now I was able to see only by the light of the moon reflecting on the snow. When I got to the top, I prayed, took a deep breath and chose another trail. About fifty yards into it I saw the lights of some cars in the distance below. I can still feel the extreme joy and relief at knowing I was going to make it out alive. Skiing as fast as I could, I finally descended the last small slope to the parking lot. Offering a prayer of gratitude, I started the car to get the heater working. Stopping at the first store I found, I bought some Gatorade. I drank one container right at the checkout register and took the other one with me. What a lesson I learned on this skiing trip! It qualified me to be listed among "Murray's Fools," and it's a story I never though I would live to tell.

While not as dramatic as the struggle for survival in Jack London's *The Call of the Wild*, *To Build a Fire* and his other stories, my brief sojourn into the crucible at the wild's edge certainly heightened my senses and called into operation all my instincts and resources for survival. All my petty and peripheral issues fell away as I was wholly engaged in the struggle for life. My inconsequential concerns, personal preferences and philosophical constructs all deferred to the immediate demands of reality.

Another verse from Teilhard de Chardin's *Hymn of the Universe* sums up the insight of my skiing trip as well as this tenth mile of my mountain retreat:

> Blessed be you, harsh matter...stubborn rock ...untamable passion: you who... by constantly shattering our mental categories, force us to go ever further and further in pursuit of the truth.

My skiing adventure left me not only with a deeper appreciation for the gift of life but also with a renewed and maturing faith. It forged a deeper connection to God, whose presence I felt within and after the struggle. And the call to venture deeper into the wilderness resonates with Teilhard's reflection:

> Purity does not lie in separation from, but in a deeper penetration into the universe. It is to be found in the love of that unique, boundless Essence which penetrates the inmost depths of all things....
>
> Son of man, bathe yourself in the ocean of matter; plunge into it where it is deepest and most violent; struggle in its currents and drink of its waters. For it cradled you long ago in your preconscious existence; and it is that ocean that will raise you up to God.

My wilderness experiences have also left with a renewed desire to defer my preferences to the way of the Spirit right in the fabric of my daily life. In a way, I want to *live* in the backcountry, take up residence in the wild, so that I might stay in contact with "that unique, boundless Essence."

I think about my experience among the indigenous Mayans in the highlands of Guatemala, a people who do live in the backcountry and who don't have a comfortable home in civilization to return to after a 12-day trek into the wild. In one of my visits, I was asked by a Mayan community living in *el campo* (the backcountry) to come and bless corn seeds that they would use for the next planting. I traveled many kilometers over bad roads to the old church. Upon arriving, I was struck by the sad condition of poverty I found. Yet my first impression was overshadowed by the warm hospitality of the men, women and children gathered inside the church. Their colorful hand-woven clothing spoke of celebration and of a vibrancy of life even in their seemingly dire circumstances. The dirt floor in the small church, about the size of a three-car garage, was covered with fresh pine needles — a wonderful symbol of the ever-green faith lived out in this community. The aroma of the pine needles joined with the smoke of burning incense and candles to give the air a sacred scent. Dim light from the candles illuminated and enhanced the people's beautiful, dark facial features.

The rituals of song and prayers began, soon followed by a procession with baskets of seeds. Several of the Elders carried to the altar-table all the seeds that were to be blessed with the holy water and incense. I was awestruck by the reverent manner in which the Mayans handled corn seeds. If even one fell to the ground, it was retrieved with great devotion. Their work-worn hands — from the demands of their primitive agriculture — were the prayerful hands of a priest holding a sacred object. And, indeed, the seed was for them the kernel of life itself.

I attempted to explain to this assembly that although we in the north have our technology and computers, they still know the secrets of nature and live close to Mother Earth. I said that someday, perhaps, we might come and ask them to teach us how to find what we have lost. We might come to learn the spiritual mysteries of a life connected to the earth, to learn about their use of medicinal herbs, their harmony with the rhythm of the seasons and natural life cycles, their sense of community, family and faith.

This was a privileged moment for me. These seeds were all that stood between them and the possibility of starvation in the next harvest season. How tenuous life is for them. I can never walk into one of our supermarkets without thinking about the great abundance of all kinds of food displayed before me, in contrast to the simple baskets of seeds I blessed in *Agua Escondita*. Our supermarkets have more food in one store than there are in most whole villages in the third world. Yet what incredible abundance is stored in the soul of those village communities. Here is a beautiful example of that soulful vitality from the journal of a travel companion of mine, Tom Benevento:

> Don German steps out of his tiny room into the awakening morning. It's 5:00 A.M. He stands in his over-stretched wool hat, layers of torn shirts and sweaters, and two pairs of pants, with the inner bright green ones showing through the holes of the blue outer pair. His dusty dark boots, like elf shoes, curl up at the toes. The sky is still slate blue with fading stars. Don German looks to the east, makes a blessing into the sky and quietly bows.

> Don German is pure Mayan Cakchiquel, just reaching his 76th year. I hear him in the early morning as I lie in bed. He goes to the washing

sink coughing and rinsing his mouth for the few teeth he has left. Then to the kitchen made of boards, adobe walls and a pitted dirt floor to start the day's fire. Singing and saying, *"Dios mi Madre"* ("God, my Mother"), he uses a small machete to split *ecoti*, a type of pitch pine, into thin slices. He places them next to the remains of last night's fire, a heap of ashes. I get up to join him with his family. Suddenly he is quiet. He smoothes out the ashes and begins a blessing to the fire, making an imprint in the soot. He says to me, "Firewood is filled with life, and it offers itself to us so that we can have life. Fire is like our brother."

While eating breakfast, Don German begins coughing hard and gasping, as if he isn't going to catch his breath. It startles me. He stops and looks up at me with a grin and says, "Maybe I'll have one more year of life, but I'm content. I'm made from God. I'm ready to be taken. This life is but a speck in time." At the end of the meal, as is the custom, he goes to each person around the fire and offers thanks, saying, *"Matiox, Dios xi-un in Cakchiquel."* Each returns the same. He says, "If we have a full meal, we give thanks. If we have only tortillas with salt, we give thanks equally for whatever is placed before us."

Don German lives simply. His heart is grateful for even the smallest things. He lives with a deep religious devotion. Each act is a religious ritual and reflects a comfortable intimacy with his God. He is content with his lot in life in a way that mirrors a deep connectedness with the natural world around him.

I am learning much from Don German and many like him in his "underdeveloped" culture, including the Gaviotas of Columbia. In his book *Gavitotas, a Village:*

To Reinvent the World, Alan Weisman tells the story of Paolo Lugari. A graduate from Bogotá's Universidad Nacional, even though he never attended classes, Lugari began working for the United Nations Food and Agricultural Organization. In 1971, together with a group of Colombian scientists, artisans, rural peasants, former street kids and Guahibo Indians, Lugari decided to set up Gaviotas. Sixteen hours from the nearest major city and accessible only by an almost impassible dirt road, it sits amid the barren, rain-leached savannas east of the Colombian Andes. Yet Gaviotas has emerged as a sustainable-environment model for the rest of the world. The creators managed to bring modern comforts to a barren area without the usual pollution and deforestation. They invented windmills light enough to convert subtle tropical breezes into energy, solar collectors that can work in the rain, pumps hooked to children's seesaws to replenish their school's water supply and soil-free systems to raise crops. Although Gaviotas families have their own kitchens, they mostly eat in an open-air dining room. A hundred-plus people gather at long tables for lentil soup, salad, rice, meat-and-potato stew, cassava and papaya juice. Vegetables, beef, pork and fish are produced there. I contrast this model of sustainable living with our conspicuous consumerism.

According to *The Global Citizen*: "Gaviotans live in peace surrounded by narcotics dealers and guerillas. They live without guns, without pesticides, willing to serve and teach all comers. They count their wealth in sun, water, and community."

There is a quality of life in backcountry places like Guatemala and Columbia that I find missing in North America. Why do so many of them smile? What hidden resources of life are they drawing from in adversity? Our postmodern world is changing rapidly. We don't have time to process the effects these changes are having on us. These backcountry places can serve as important reminders about essential values that are quickly disappearing: the values of community, family, closeness with the earth, sustainable living, gratefulness, gladness and joy in living. A core tenet of Liberation Theology is that sometimes the political centers of power and learning can be confounded by persons or cultures on the margins. Jesus certainly understood this reality. Coming from Nazareth, a backcountry place, the people sought him out for his wisdom rather than pursuing the teachings of the learned and powerful from Jerusalem. Can the powerful be humble enough to learn from the marginal?

What calls me into the wild? What keeps luring me into the backcountry places of the Adirondack Mountains and Guatemala? What keeps inviting me to experience the sometimes-harsh realities of backcountry life? Though this tenth mile hike has thrown much insight into these questions, they still keep circulating within as I head back toward base camp. Indeed, the Adirondack backcountry is for me the spiritual desert place of Hosea where God speaks deeply to my heart. I come here to shed the accumulated skins of the values of our fashion-conscious, consumer-oriented society. It is here that I can examine what baggage I have accumulated, and, like the Huaorani, look at what I need to unpack so that I can travel lightly.

Backcountry experiences here in the Adirondacks or in Guatemala are *awakening* experiences for me. I need to experience sudden downpours of rain, walking in ankle-deep mud or being crammed on a Guatamalan public bus with a 150 other people. I need to wear the same clothing three or four days running and to experience the endless delays and the constant surprises and changes in plans that remind me how one should be prepared for the unexpected in life. I need to endure the crucible of some discomfort — from mosquitoes to the pain of blistered feet — so that I will not live under the illusion that I am in control. I need reminders that life in the real world isn't lived with tidy and tightly efficient schedules. In backcountry territory, scales fall off my eyes, and I see that harsher realities are filled with paradoxes — like finding abundant life among the poor — and with miracles of a human-kind, where God is tasted in the bread of daily life.

I respond to the call of the wild because I feel there is something inside me that never wants to be tamed. When we let that wild element within us become domesticated, the fire of passion burns out and we die spiritually. Backcountry places remove illusions and put us in touch with the untamable spirit within so we can feel that we are still *alive*, and not just living.

Almost without my notice, I've made my way through the "deep" of this backcountry and circled my way toward my base camp for the night. As I approach my campsite, I'm aware of how I want to live a more congruent life — my daily choices and decisions in concert with my deeper truths. I want to be in touch with my "truth force."

With this desire reverberating in my heart, I set down my daypack and take off my hiking boots. It feels good to rest. I brew some hot tea and write down some points for reflection before supper:

♦ How can I maintain my connection to the wilderness — and, more importantly, my relationship to the "unique, boundless Essence" — in the midst of my comfortable, civilized existence?

♦ How do I habitually resist hearing the call of the wild — and of God luring me into the wilderness?

♦ How can I continue to dive deeper into the "ocean of matter" and into my pursuit of the truth?

- What does the lesson of Don German teach me about how to live my daily life?

- How can I deepen my solidarity with the poor and marginalized who *live* in "the wilderness"?

- Where are the backcountry places (and peoples) in which I can seek out wisdom and learning right in the midst of my life?

- Meditate more on Jesus, who was drawn deep into the wilderness and who chose, for most of his life, to take up residence in the backcountry.

- What aspects of my life feed the need for wildness?

Mile Eleven

Meltdown and a Spirituality for the Next Mile

As profound as yesterday's trek deep into the backcountry was, and as perfect a day for backpacking as this is — with its bright sun, deep blue sky and dry air — I am, nevertheless, feeling a strong need to end this trek. I want to hike out and head home. It's not just the accumulation of irritating discomfort factors, including grimy clothing, salty skin, matted hair and a couple of nasty blisters. It's also a stifling weariness — a low-grade exhaustion coupled with a compelling longing for home and companionship.

I've reached the meltdown point that's similar to what marathon runners describe as "hitting the wall." They say it can happen as many as six times during the 26-mile run, but the toughest wall hits about 20 miles into the marathon, in the final approach to the finish line. Its spiritual counterpart is the dark night of the soul. When in an extreme state of being worn down physically or spiritually, one is faced with the choice either "to keep on keeping on" or to pack it up and quit.

I think of the many real life situations like that, whether a job, marriage, friendship, career or ministry. Like the start of my mountain retreat, we initially enter these situations with energy and enthusiasm, accepting the challenges. After the honeymoon period, we often proceed in stride for some time before we begin to notice a change. The luster is lacking. Routine sets in, and we face the harsh reality of our life choice. Instead of living in the dizzying heights of newness, we feel pressed down to the ground, stuck in place; everything feels so "heavy" with the responsibility of it all. Lightness and laughter are rare or missing. We wonder if we have the inner resources to cope. We find ourselves asking, "What did I get myself into?" Our capacities seem stretched to the breaking point.

As I break camp this morning and take to the trail for this eleventh mile, I recall my solo 8-day, 95-mile trek on the Wonderland Trail around the base of Mt. Rainier one summer. It stands out as the most demanding physical challenge I've ever faced. It too started out on a beautiful day luminous with sunshine. The mountain stood silently and majestically against the deep blue sky. Snow-covered glacial ice blanketed Rainier's steep slopes that converged to a point 14,000 feet above the earth. Playful marmots would occasionally stand up on hind legs and look out over a sea of flowering blue lupines at hikers passing by on the trails. By the second day, however, everything changed. The sky turned gray, light rain began to fall, and for the next five days, rain, fog and clouds covered the mountain, concealing her beauty from view. I wasn't really prepared for the extreme altitude changes either — two to three thousand feet each day was not uncommon. Moreover, the hiker has to pack everything in on his or her back: the food, tent, sleeping bag, clothing and water. It was grueling. The only flat places were the few footbridges I crossed. The steep grade caused blisters to form on my toes and the bottom of my soles. My knee joints constantly ached. By the time I reached the Carbon River post, about halfway around the mountain, I was in an extreme state, physically. I wondered if I was going to be able to finish the trek.

As I now make my way out of the Upper Twin Brooks area on this eleventh mile hike, I feel like a mountain climber who experiences the pull of gravity more strongly on the steeper part of the slope, when nearing the top. Frequent stops to catch one's breath are needed. One's steady stride now becomes a one-step-at-a-time process. With the slow progress, the climber has to look beyond the struggle and apply the force of will in order to persevere to the end. It's not the time to turn back, when you're just short of the top. Yet sometimes in life, no incentive seems strong enough to keep us going.

Perhaps my biggest spiritual crisis happened after I had been ordained about 15 years and had reached my forty-fifth year of age. I'd been named director of a Spanish apostolate that took me from an affluent suburban community to minister to farm workers and various Hispanic groups, some recently immigrated to the United States. I was excited by the vibrant life of these peoples, their foods, festivals and cultural richness. I felt very much accepted by them, even though I was struggling to learn the language and culture. Though things moved slowly at first, in time our pastoral team put into place programs such as parenting skills, conflict resolution and English as a second language. Councils were created for community input, and we even formed a non-profit corporation that received a grant to build farm-worker housing. This, however, did not please the larger local community, many of whom did not want "them" (the farm workers) living in their community. It got ugly as town people shouted us down at town meetings, and zoning variances were denied. The Department of Housing and Urban Development (HUD) got involved, and ultimately the New York State Court of Appeals. There was advocacy on the behalf of the Hispanic community in the Federal Immigration Service, the court system, housing authorities, health clinics and school districts. I was more and more absorbed by the social work, grant writing, budgets and the growing demands of this ministry. Added to that, I was beginning to feel overwhelmed by the many social and economic difficulties of some of the community members. It seemed like there were fewer resources and larger problems. Moreover, we were now serving communities in three different counties, and I would drive a 90-mile loop each Sunday for liturgies. After seven years, I began to feel tired of it. It wasn't the people but the administrative responsibilities that were wearing me down. I felt more and more frustrated with the obstacles these people faced in their efforts to get ahead. I began to gain weight, and for a brief time I began smoking again. Even more distressing was the reality of being mired in a dark night of the soul. I wasn't happy with the way I was functioning in my ministry. Even the thought of ministry brought a sense of dread. I realized I was just going through the motions, without passion or life. It was total burnout.

I applied for a sabbatical and was given a year to retreat, recreate and enjoy new learning experiences in Boston. I look back on that time and wonder how I got through each day. I have no explanation, except for the prayers, support and guidance of so many friends, who were true spiritual beacons in my dark night. Yet from this side of that burnout crisis, I can recognize within my darkness the subtle working of the Spirit, enabling a deeper layer of faith to emerge in my life.

Curiously, as I think back on my Mt. Rainier trek, there *was* something that kept me going. It was the iridescent glow of some stray flowering blue lupine in the early morning fog. It couldn't see the "big things," like the mountain peaks, but as my attention was drawn to small clusters of this tiny flower, my mind and spirit were refreshed and rejuvenated. Lupines kept appearing before me on the side of the trails, displaying a special beauty in the murky morning that couldn't be seen in the bright sunlight. It made me understand the stories of heroic survivors like Victor Frankl and Etty Hillesum, who were forced to endure the extreme conditions of Nazi concentration camps. While imprisoned behind barbed wire in the stark barracks at Westerbork, Etty described a sky full of birds and the purple lupine standing up so regally and peacefully in the midst of the squalor. When asked how she could think of flowers in that hell, she replied that they were just as real as the misery she saw each day. That's it!

Sometimes when we are expecting something big or dramatic to solve our problems, instead our deepest resources are triggered by something small and almost inconspicuous. A parent might be brought to an extreme state by the uncontrollable crying of a baby. Yet in that momentary pause when the baby stops crying and smiles, it becomes possible for the weary parent to make it through the night. It was a small purple lupine that sustained Etty Hillesum in her momentous ordeal and some blue lupine that kept me going on the Wonderland Trail. I think that's what is meant when Scripture talks about faith the size of a mustard seed that can move a mountain.

Buoyed by these reflections, it dawns on me as I near the end of this 12-mile backpacking trek, that it has indeed become a pilgrimage. Whereas a tourist likes to travel in comfort, a pilgrim accepts the element of physical hardship built into the journey. Pilgrims carry a load and walk long distances to their spiritual destination. In an article entitled "Tourist or Pilgrim?" Paul Robichaud says:

> A tourist is a traveler who seeks to replicate
> in a foreign land much of his or her own world.

Cameras and souvenirs provide the means fondly to remember the trip. A pilgrim, by distinction, is a traveler in search of something outside of the familiar. Pilgrimage was and is at its core a journey into the unknown. A pilgrim goes in search of the holy away from the structures of everyday life. For medieval Christians, to make a single pilgrimage in one's lifetime was considered a great religious accomplishment, as it still is today for Muslims who journey to Mecca. Tourists are on a schedule and must keep to their itinerary. Sometimes the pace is frenzied. Many times the spiritual experience is not included. The pilgrimage is out to seek the spiritual richness of the site traveled to. There is a spiritual richness in what they are encountering.

Linda Davidson defines a pilgrimage as "a journey to a place that has spiritual significance for the journeyer." The Adirondacks are that for me. During my days of solitude here, quintessential spiritual questions have kept coming to the surface of my mind like bubbles rising from the bottom of a pond. This has become something of a vision quest, a consecrated search for the Holy Grail. Even in the midst of a meltdown, the expansiveness of the sky and grandeur of these majestic mountains have created in me the spiritual spaciousness I've needed to review my quintessential life questions.

A few hours into today's trek, I decide to sit on one of the large boulders on the riverbank and enjoy some refreshing water and warm sunshine. The sound of the water flowing over the rocks is as soothing as any symphony. My tired muscles are grateful for the break. A Mountain Maple next to me offers its gift of mottled colors with her last few clinging leaves. I accept graciously and touch one of the leaves to feel its texture. This leaf will no doubt be carried by the river to a place far beyond, completing its life journey. As I visually follow the Opalescent coursing to its confluence with its larger sister, the Hudson, I wonder if it's my destiny to be drawn into a greater life beyond this earthly span. I believe it is. The day's sunlight is now stronger and warmer, corresponding to my inner illuminations and stream of consciousness that come and go with the river flow. Though it may not be the kind of endorphin rush that often accompanies breaking through a "wall," I am experiencing a higher level of energy in this soothing yet expansive space. Spiritually refreshed, I put my tired legs to the test by standing and lifting my backpack to continue the hike out.

Aware that it is ultimately my faith that sustains me on the journey, and aware that my faith is nourished by my spirituality, I turn my attention to a question that has been a constant companion on this mountain retreat: the very notion of spirituality itself. I've noticed a shift in my understanding of spirituality. It is reflected in an African tribal elder's response to a question asked by a Western missionary, "Where does your spirituality come from?" The elder answered, "From the soles of my feet." In the background I hear Yahweh's voice in the burning bush instructing Moses to take his sandals off because he is standing on holy ground. For the last several days I feel I have been walking on holy ground, experiencing my spirituality from the "soles of my feet." Author Mary Vineyard writes: "But I swear I've seen angels cry from envy because we can walk barefoot in the grass."

This journey has helped me understand that my spirituality rests on three pillars. The first is *incarnational,* rooted in the awareness that religious experiences are mediated through our senses and that all our senses are in contact with this expansive universe. Harmonizing with the poetry of Teilhard de Chardin, one of Edna St. Vincent Millay's sonnets says, "O world, I cannot hold thee close enough." Deep ecologist Thomas Berry, a Passionist priest, chimes in, saying that the earth is our primary revelatory environment. Though the Bible's revelation covered over two thousand years, creation has been speaking of God for five billion years.

Other spiritual writers like Matthew Fox, Jim Conlon and Miriam Therese McGillis have helped us reclaim a creation-centered spirituality. It's an organic type of spirituality that overcomes some of the dualisms of the past. It emphasizes community and a mutuality of relationships over and above patriarchal and hierarchal structures. Rather than emphasizing original sin, it recovers the original blessing given creation in Genesis when "God saw that it was all so good" (Genesis 1: 31). And that blessing extends to the entire universe, not just to human beings. A creation-centered spirituality highlights the sacramentality of all things.

As I hike, carrying this notion in my mental backpack, I recall a retreat given by Fr. William McNamara. His term *earthy mystic* has remained with me through the years. In ancient mystery religions the word *mystical* meant *hidden*. It referred to rituals that were hidden from the uninitiated. The early Christians believed that divine realities were experienced in the symbols of ritual contact (later called sacraments). Christians were thus able to know God through tangible experience. Earthy mystics are those who directly sense the sacred veiled in all material reality. As McNamara says, earthy mystics take "long loving looks at the real." Nikos Kazantzakis, a great and passionate poetic writer, points us to earthy-mysticism when he describes St. Francis:

> Each dawn, when the birds begin to sing again, or at midday when he plunged into the cooling shade of the forest, or at night, sitting in the moonlight or beneath the stars, he would shudder from inexpressible joy and gaze at me,

his eyes filled with tears, "What miracles these are, Brother Leo!" he would say. "And He who created such beauty — what can we call Him?"

Seeing like this gives fresh meaning to the text, "The Word became flesh and pitched His tent among us" (John 1: 14).

Brother David Steindl-Rast advances an earthy mysticism with his notion of *sensuous asceticism*. Using this scandalous-sounding term, he rescues asceticism from all its negative connotations of penance, mortification, self-torment and unhealthy attitudes about our bodies and the created world. Authentic asceticism is self-denial only in the sense that we refrain from self-sabotaging behaviors that prevent our truest selves from shining through. In the process, asceticism heightens our appreciation of the natural world and its gifts and leads us to a truer, deeper self-respect. Steindl-Rast teaches that the senses are a source of sensuous delight that can lift us upward to an inner spiritual height. In *Walden* Henry David Thoreau concludes his chapter titled "Higher Laws" with this scene:

> John Farmer sat at his door one September evening, after a hard day's work.... He had not attended to the train of his thoughts long when he heard someone playing on a flute, and that sound harmonized with his mood.... But the notes of the flute came home to his ears out of a different sphere from that he worked in, and suggested work for certain faculties which slumbered in him.... A voice said to him, — Why do you stay here and live this mean moiling life, when a glorious existence is possible for you? — But how to come out of this condition and actually migrate thither? All that he could think of was to practice some new austerity, to let his mind descend into his body and redeem it, and to treat

himself with ever increasing respect.

Earthy mystics and sensuous ascetics have a sense of the *mirandum,* a fascination with the beauty and mystery of reality. Earthy mystics live deeply and passionately. Theirs is not a *fuga mundi,* a flight from the world, but, rather, a deeper plunging into the world.

The second pillar of my spirituality involves living *compassionately* as well as passionately. In fact, it flows out of a passionate "love of that unique, boundless Essence which penetrates the inmost depths of all things," as Teilhard says. The word compassion comes from the Latin *con*, meaning "with," and *patio*, "to suffer." The "suffering with" of compassion could be compared to a mother's feeling for her child; it's a womb-like love for others. A spirituality of compassion draws us to all other living beings. It's consciously cultivating concern and love for others. As this spiritual consciousness deepens, it's like the ripple effect of a stone thrown into the still waters of a pond; the circle continues to widen until the shore is reached. As we grow in compassion, our feelings for the suffering of others continues to broaden. It includes enemies as well as friends, all other sentient life forms — animals and plants — as well as all other human beings sharing life with us on this good earth.

My third spiritual pillar is the practice of *solidarity*. Dorotheus of Gaza, a sixth-century monk, used this analogy to describe a spirituality of solidarity: Take a compass and draw a circle. The circle is the world and God is the center. To move toward God, you move from the circumference of the circle into the center. As you move toward the center, you discover that all the lines drawn from the circumference to the center — yours as well as those of all peoples — are drawn close together. The closer you move to God, the closer you move toward others. So simple a metaphor, yet so profound a truth.

Leonardo Boff, a leader in the Liberation Theology

movement, writes of a personal vision:

> In those days, the Christ of Corcovado, overlooking the city of San Sebastin de Rio de Janeiro, shivered and came to life. Once cement and rock, He became flesh and blood. He extended his arms, reaching for the city and the world, opened his mouth, and said: I feel pity for you, millions and millions of sisters and brothers, my little ones, driven off your land, solitary, hidden in jungles, piled up at the borders, fallen along so many paths, with no Samaritan to save you.... Blessed be you all, the poor, hungry, ailing, and the hopeless. My Father (sic), giver of life, holds you in His Heart. He will inaugurate His Kingdom of life, of justice, of tenderness and you will be its first inhabitants.... Woe to you owners of power ...there is only one path for salvation for you, just one: join in solidarity with the struggles of the oppressed who search for bread, freedom, tenderness and beauty, not only for themselves. Take on the project of the poor, which will be tranformative for you, and there may be more life and freedom for all.

Some of the spiritual systems of the past were intensely individualistic. They were *vertical* and not *horizontal*. One's relationship with God was everything. One's relationship with others was peripheral at best. A journey to the mountaintop was often used as a metaphor to describe this *vertical* quest. Reaching the top, one would transcend all human misery and leave behind all worldly longings. "The only problem with this metaphor," says Bhiksuni Pema Chodon, "is that we leave all the others behind — our drunken brothers, our schizophrenic sister, our tormented animals and friends. Their suffering continues, unrelieved by our personal escape."

There is a legend about a man who was fed up with all the brokenness and confusion and troubles of his town. So he decided to flee his world, with all its pain and problems, to go live on the top of the great mountain. There, he thought, he would be in a place of rare and purified air and sunlight. There, he thought, he could live in peace with God. And so, he began his journey of ascending the mountain of God. After many days of rigorous ascent, he met a friend coming down the mountain. The climber's friend asked where he was going, and he replied, "I'm going to the mountaintop to live with God and be at peace." His friend replied, "I've been to the top of the mountain, and God isn't there. God left the mountaintop to live in the valley among all the humans."

The two main New Testament events underscore God's solidarity with us: Jesus' birth and his death. These two events flesh out the statement, "He came and pitched His tent among us." God is not the solitary mountaintop dweller living above the valley of our daily human experience. Our God is a God of solidarity who has moved from the mountaintop, through the desert, from the Ark, from the Temple built by human hands and now dwells in the temple of our common humanity. What a consoling thought! In Jesus, God lived our ordinary life, lived in solidarity with us. This is not only an approachable God, but a God who takes the initiative to approach us. This is a God with human skin. An incarnation! As close as you can get!

As I descend this mountain at the end of my backpacking retreat, I'm struck by how fluid is the relationship among these spiritual pillars. The reality of the incarnate God is at the base of all three. As I come down from the mountaintop, I'm also grateful for — and draw from — the courage, clarity, peace and all the inner resources I've gained here that can make life in the valley transformative rather than oppressive.

With all these reflections reverberating in my mind and soul, I pass an old tote road and approach a swampy area with a corduroy portion of trail (a section built with cut logs laid horizontally on the trail for easier passing through wet sections). I walk over the log and plank bridge that spans Lake Jimmy. Soon I reach the small suspension footbridge over the Hudson River.

It's day's end. Though I have less than a quarter of a mile to travel to the parking lot, I decide to set up camp for the night here where the Hudson and the Opalescent converge. I want to let my thoughts rest in solitude one last night, to "sleep over" the whole twelve miles of my mountain retreat. Watching and listening to the river, I remember a line from *Siddhartha* by Hermann Hesse: "The river is always the same and always changing." This is a good summary of my experience here. I take my leather tramp journal out to write a few final reflections for meditation:

♦ Ask the environment of this eleventh mile about what lesson I still need to learn here that I can carry back to my daily life.

♦ What spiritual qualities and resources might I cultivate to address meltdown/burnout before it happens?

♦ Can I be open to God's presence — pray — right in the midst of meltdown?

♦ List two or three spiritually sound disciplines to practice each day to deepen my sense of passion, compassion and solidarity.

♦ How will my spiritual pillars translate into concern for the environment and justice issues; how will living them contribute to a more loving and peaceful world?

Mile Twelve

Journey's End

The low, lyrical voice of the Opalescent has been like a lullaby as it's flowed over the rocks of the riverbed throughout the night. She and her sisters, Hanging Spear Falls and the Hudson River, have been good company throughout my journey. Having broken camp one last time, I now take leave of my water companions as I cross over a short footbridge. I follow the crushed tailings on this old road, and before long I reach the parking lot where I left my car. I let my backpack slide down to the ground, lean it against the car and begin fumbling for the keys in a side pocket of the pack. Voilà! Here they are. As I open the door and trunk, I sit quietly for a moment before changing clothes and kicking off my hiking boots. Draining the last few ounces of water from my water bottle, I reflect on what a great trek this has been. Still, I am ready to pack it in and get home to a hot shower, a comfortable bed, real food and friends.

I came into the woods without my interior compass locked onto magnetic north. I didn't know just where I would be led. I wasn't sure what kind of topography of the soul I would travel over. I am leaving, however, with a better sense of my spiritual map. Having wrestled with my angel, I realize that the trail of life is lived more like a zigzag pattern than a straight line. One has to have faith during life's transitions and trust that a providential love is at work; one has to trust that all *will* be well. A passage from Romans reminds me that "For those who love God all things work for their good" (Romans 8: 28).

I entered this trip with some quintessential questions. I still carry them. While not fully resolved, they seem less opaque — more transparent — than when I began. I feel content in the midst of the uncertainty. I am more accepting of not being in control, more grounded in the wisdom of insecurity. Some of the questions in my quest have found enough gravity to reach ground zero, the place of inner clarity and peace. Other reflections along the way were like flat stones skipping across a pond, just touching the surface before coming to rest. On future treks I will plunge into those questions for a deeper awareness about spirituality, about my life choices and about where life is for me. But even within the fabric of my daily life I will take to heart Thoreau's tenet to "live more deliberately."

Even as I move my stuff around in the trunk, my mind continues to revolve around this trip. I recall a scene from Dostoyevsky's *The Brothers Karamazov*. Aloyosha falls into a trance at the death of his teacher Father Zossima. Upon returning to consciousness, he cries out, "Someone visited my soul at that hour!" That expresses my feelings about this 12-day hike. It was an experience of the graced wilderness Hosea speaks about: "I am going to lure her and lead her out into the wilderness and speak to her heart" (Hosea 2: 16). I feel that the Holy Spirit has visited me on this pilgrimage trek and left me with a feeling I can only describe as a peaceful restlessness. It's not so much that I see different things but that I see things differently. I have a greater capacity to look upon the ordinary in an extraordinary way. In that light, I'm encouraged by the experience of Thomas Merton:

> In Louisville, at the corner of Fourth and Walnut, in the center of the shopping district, I was suddenly overwhelmed with the realization that I loved all those people, that they were mine and I theirs, that we could not be alien to one another even though we were total strangers. It was like waking from a dream of separateness,

of spurious self-isolation in a special world, the world of renunciation and supposed holiness. The whole illusion of a separate holy existence is a dream.... Then it was as if I suddenly saw the secret beauty of their hearts ...the core of their reality, the person that each one is in God's eyes. If only we could see each other that way all the time. There would be no more war, no more hatred, no more cruelty, no more greed.

There is a common expectation when one retreats from the work-a-day world that one will return with new insights about one's world. Yet Merton's mystical experience occurred on a busy city street, not in his hermitage. At the same time, his solitary experience was like a reservoir; he carried the flowing grace that was collected in his hermitage to the corner of Fourth and Walnut. Similarly, I trust that my mountain retreat will help me continue to see some things differently in my busy life in the city.

My gear now stowed away, I molt out of my old worn clothing. I feel transformed by the clean cotton shirt, pants and socks. The weather is changing, and it looks like it might rain soon. I welcome the change because the sound of falling rain will deepen my sense of peace. My state of being is well described by the Hebrew word for peace. *Shalom* is more than the absence of war. It's more than being at rest, more than an absence of disorder. In fact, it's a dynamic state; it includes a higher degree of energy than the normal conflict, stress and chaos in life. It is harmony within oneself, with God, with others and with all creation. It connotes just and right relationships with all life. Even though I've been apart from others during this trek, I somehow feel closer to them. I have hiked in solitude but have a deeper sense of community and solidarity that now includes all the natural life around me: the trees, stones, rivers and forest creatures. The Spirit has used it all in restoring me to a new level of healing and wholeness.

This mountain trek has given me the opportunity to explore many valleys and peaks of my 58 years of life and 28 years of active ministry. There is gratitude for the rich and diverse life experiences. Even though some of my views are in conflict with official church positions, policies and teachings, I've gained insights during these 12 miles on how ministry has been a deep and rich gift in my life. I know it will affect the way I minister to others in the future.

The time has now come to move from the ridge view back into the valleys. At almost the very moment I start the car, rain begins to fall. I see this not only as a sign of closure for this mountain retreat but also as a sign that I will soon be enjoying one of life's simple pleasures: a hot shower. As the gossamer threads of my daily life and relationships draw me back to the civilized world, I hope to pack out a greater awareness of others' needs. I also carry back a commitment to lifestyle choices that are more in line with the needs of our precious natural environment. Beyond that, I want to be less serious and have a lot more fun.

The ultimate test of the depth and duration of this experience will come when I return to the busy market-place of my life. The measuring stick will be how I face the daily challenges, the unexpected interruptions, the latest global tragedy, the conspicuous consumerism, the blatant injustices. Part of me always tries to escape hard reality, but this retreat has given me resources to handle it all differently. A rabbinical story speaks of this fresh perspective:

> In the hiddenness of time there was a poor man who left his village, weary of life, longing for a place where he could escape all the struggles of this earth. He set out in search of a magical city

— the heavenly city of his dreams, where all things would be perfect. He walked all day and by dusk found himself in a forest, where he decided to spend the night. Eating the crust of bread he had brought, he said his prayers and, just before going to sleep, placed his shoes in the center of the path, pointing them in the direction he would continue the next morning. Little did he imagine that while he slept, a practical joker would come along and turn his shoes around, pointing them back in the direction from which he had come.

The next morning, in all the innocence of folly, he got up, gave thanks to the Lord of the Universe and started on his way again in the direction that his shoes pointed. For a second time he walked all day, and toward evening he finally saw the magical city in the distance. It wasn't as large as he had expected. As he got closer, it looked curiously familiar. But he pressed on, found a street much like his own, knocked on a familiar door, and greeted the family he found there, and he lived happily ever after in the magical city of his dreams.

I look in the rearview mirror and catch a fleeting glimpse of the old MacIntyre Iron Works blast furnace and the old, abandoned village of Adirondack fading from view. I am headed in a new direction. As I do, I pass these leather tramp reflections on to other spiritual pilgrims in the spirit of a beggar, simply telling about the last place I got fed. I leave you with a question and a quote: *Where is life for you?*

> We shall not cease from exploring
> and the end of all our exploring
> will be to arrive where we started
> and know the place for the first time.
> —T.S. Eliot

Recommended Reading

BOFF, LEONARDO AND ELIZONDO, VIRGIL. *Ecology and Poverty,* New York: Orbis Books, 1995.

GOTTLIEB, ROGER, S. *A Spirituality of Resistance,* New York: Crossroad, 1999.

HERTSGAARD, MARK. *Earth Odyssey,* New York: Broadway Books, 1998.

HESCHEL, ABRAHAM. *I Asked for Wonder: A Spiritual Anthology*, Samuel H. Dresner, ed., New York: Crossroad, 1993.

KURTZ, ERNEST AND KETCHAM. *The Spirituality of Imperfection*, New York: Bantam Books, 1994.

MC FAGUE, SALLY. *Super, Natural Christians: How We Should Love Nature,* Minneapolis: Fortress Press, 1997.

OLIVER, MARY. *New and Selected Poems of Mary Oliver*, Boston: Beacon Press, 1993.

O' MURCHU, DIARMUID. *Reclaiming Spirituality,* New York: Crossroad, 1997.

RASMUSSEN, LARRY, L. *Earth Community Earth Ethics,* New York: Orbis Books, 1996.

ROSENBLATT, ROGER. *Consuming Desires, Consumption, Culture, and the Pursuit of Happiness,* Washington, D.C.: Island Press, 1999.

SMITH, PAMELA. *Environmental Ethics?* Mahwah, N.J.: Paulist Press, 1997.

STEINDL-RAST, BR. DAVID. *Gratefulness: The Heart of Prayer*, Mahwah, N.J.: Paulist Press, 1990.

SWIMME, BRIAN AND BERRY, THOMAS. *The Universe Story: From the Primordial Flaring Forth to the Ecozoic Era*, San Francisco: HarperCollins, 1992.

THOREAU, HENRY DAVID. *Walden and Other Writings,* New York: Bantam Books, 1982.

WATERMAN, LAURA AND GUY. *Forest and Crag,* Boston: Appalachian Mountain Club, 1989.

WEISMEN, ALAN. *Gaviotas, A Village to Reinvent the World,* White River Junction, Ver.: Chelsea Green Publishing Company, 1998.